The Story of the Book

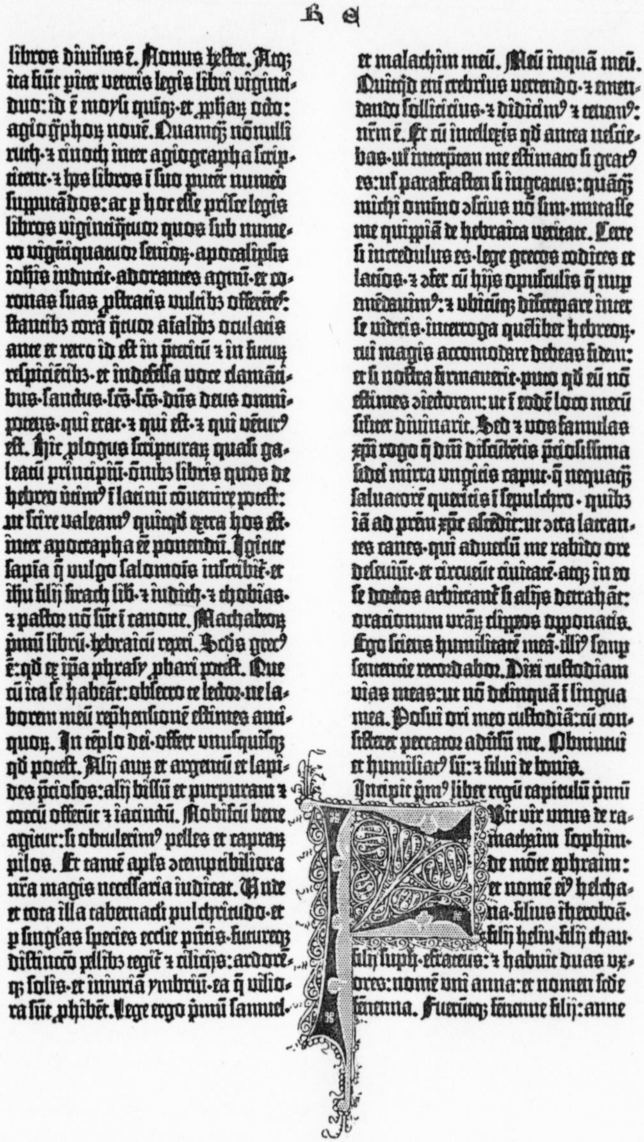

R E

libros divisus est. Nonus hester. Atque
ita fiunt pariter veteris legis libri viginti-
duo: id est moysi quinque, et prophetarum octo:
agiographorum novem. Quamquam nonnulli
ruth et cinoth inter agiographa scrip-
titent: et hos libros in suo putent numero
supputandos: ac per hoc esse prisce legis
libros vigintiquatuor quos sub numero vigintiquatuor seniorum apocalipsis
iohannis inducit adorantes agnum et co-
ronas suas prostratis vultibus offerentes:
stantibus coram quatuor animalibus oculatis
ante et retro id est in preteritum et in futurum
respicientibus et indefessa voce clamanti-
bus sanctus sanctus sanctus dominus deus omni-
potens qui erat et qui est et qui venturus
est. Hic prologus scripturarum quasi ga-
leatum principium omnibus libris quos de
hebreo vertimus in latinum convenire potest:
ut scire valeamus quicquid extra hos est
inter apocrypha esse ponendum. Igitur
sapientia que vulgo salomonis inscribitur et
iesu filii sirach liber et iudith et thobias
et pastor non sunt in canone. Machabeorum
primum librum hebraicum reperi. Secundus grecus
est: quod ex ipsa phrasi probari potest. Que
cum ita se habeant: obsecro te lector ne la-
borem meum reprehensionem estimes anti-
quorum. In templo dei offert unusquisque
quod potest. Alii aurum et argentum et lapi-
des preciosos: alii bissum et purpuram et
coccum offerunt et iacinctum. Nobiscum bene
agitur: si obtulerimus pelles et caprarum
pilos. Et tamen apostolus contemptibiliora
nostra magis necessaria iudicat. Unde
et tota illa tabernaculi pulchritudo et
per singulas species ecclesie presentis futureque
distinctio pellibus tegitur et ciliciis: ardorem-
que solis et iniuriam ymbrium ea que vilio-
ra sunt prohibent. Lege ergo primum samuel-
et malachim meum. Meum inquam meum.
Quicquid enim crebrius vertendo et emen-
dando sollicitius et didicimus et tenemus:
nostrum est. Et cum intellexeris quod antea nescie-
bas: vel interpretem me estimato si gratus
es: vel parafrasten si ingratus: quamquam
michi omnino conscius non sim mutasse
me quippiam de hebraica veritate. Certe
si incredulus es: lege grecos codices et
latinos et confer cum hiis opusculis que nuper
emendavimus: et ubicumque discrepare inter
se videris: interroga quemlibet hebreorum
cui magis accommodare debeas fidem:
et si nostra firmaverit: puto quod eum non
estimes coniectorem: ut in eodem loco mecum
similiter divinarit. Sed et vos famulas
christi rogo que domini discumbentis preciosissima
fidei mirra ungitis caput: que nequaquam
salvatorem queritis in sepulchro: quibus
iam ad patrem christus ascendit: ut contra latran-
tes canes qui adversum me rabido ore
deseviunt et circueunt civitatem: atque in eo
se doctos arbitrantur si aliis detrahant:
orationum vestrarum clipeos opponatis.
Ego sciens humilitatem meam: illius semper
sententie recordabor. Dixi custodiam
vias meas: ut non delinquam in lingua
mea. Posui ori meo custodiam: cum con-
sisteret peccator adversum me. Obmutui
et humiliatus sum: et silui de bonis.
Incipit primus liber regum capitulum primum
Fuit vir unus de ra-
mathaim sophim
de monte ephraim:
et nomen eius helcha-
na filius ieroboam
filii heliu filii thau
filii suph ephrateus: et habuit duas ux-
ores: nomen uni anna: et nomen secun-
de fenenna. Fueruntque fenenne filii: anne

A PAGE FROM THE GUTENBERG BIBLE

The Story of the Book

by

AGNES ALLEN

with drawings by

AGNES *and* JACK ALLEN

FABER AND FABER
24 Russell Square
London

*First published in mcmlii
by Faber and Faber Limited
24 Russell Square London W.C.1
Second impression mcmliii
Printed in Great Britain by
Latimer Trend & Co Ltd Plymouth
All rights reserved*

To

JACK

who loves books

Contents

Contents

Illustrations

Drawings in the Text

Drawings in the text

CHAPTER I

*

Man Begins to Write

———————————————————

Can you imagine the world without any books in it at all? Nowadays we all use books in one way or another, either at school, or in our work, or for pleasure. Even people who are not very fond of reading have to use catalogues, time-tables, dictionaries, and books of that kind. Yet men lived on earth for many thousands of years before they had anything that could be called a book at all, and for many more thousands of years before the kind of book we know to-day appeared.

Before people could make any kind of book they had to learn how to write their thoughts and ideas down in some way so that other people could understand what they meant. To-day we have a sign for each separate sound we make when we speak. As you know, we call the signs letters, and the twenty-six letters form what we call the 'alphabet'. By joining the letters together in different ways we can write down the sound of every word we speak, and anyone who has learnt how to read, and who understands our language, will know what we mean.

This seems quite simple and natural to us because we are so used to it, but human beings took thousands of years to develop an alphabet. Before that, when they wanted to write something, they had to do it in a way that we should find very difficult and uncertain.

You see, long before people could write they could draw and paint. Pictures that prehistoric men painted 50,000 years ago have been found on the walls of caves. They are drawings of the animals the men hunted for food, long before they knew anything about farming or how to grow crops, and very fine drawings some of them are.

We do not know why the cave-pictures were made, but we think they may have had something to do with religion, or a belief in magic. Perhaps the men who painted the pictures were regarded as magicians or priests, and by painting the

Drawings by cavemen

pictures they were supposed to be helping the tribe to be successful in its hunting. In a way they were writing a message in pictures on the wall, perhaps a kind of prayer that there might be plenty of animals to hunt so that the people would not starve.

It is natural for people who know nothing about the alphabet, but who want to make a record of something, or to send messages to one another, to do it by drawing little pictures.

14

The very earliest writings we know anything about were in the form of pictures, and it is from picture-writing that the different alphabets of the world gradually developed.

One difficulty about sending messages by means of pictures is that people don't always draw things in the same way. Another is that the person who receives the message, even if he can see what the objects are meant to be, may still not understand what the writer meant. Kipling has an amusing story among his *Just-so Stories* about a little prehistoric girl who 'drew' a message for her mother, and got a passing stranger to deliver it at her cave. But the mother completely misunderstood the message, with painful results for the stranger.

Kipling's story, of course, was one which he made up himself, but a Greek historian named Herodotus tells us about a King of Persia named Darius, who misunderstood a message 'written' in pictures. Darius invaded the country of the Scythians, and a Scythian herald brought him a message from his master. It was a drawing of a bird, a frog, a mouse, and three arrows. Darius puzzled over the message and finally decided that it meant that the Scythians were willing to hand over their land and their water (the frog and the mouse) and were going to fly before the arrows of the Persians. Perhaps this was an example of what we now call 'wishful thinking'. That night the Scythians attacked, and later Darius discovered that the message really meant that unless the Persians could fly away like birds, or burrow into the earth like mice, or hide in swamps like frogs, they would never escape from the arrows of the Scythians.

Because pictures could easily be misunderstood, people who communicated with each other in this way soon learnt to make their little pictures very simple, and to draw each object in the same way every time—to 'standardize' the drawings, as we should probably say now. Often they would draw only part of the object, such as a pair of horns to represent a cow, or a bow and arrow to represent a hunter, and so long as they all did the same thing there would be no misunderstanding.

It is fairly easy to make a simple little drawing to represent an actual object that can be seen, such as a bird, a tent, a leaf, a man. And it's not very difficult to think out a way of representing such a thing as water by drawing a wavy line. But it is not so easy to represent abstract things—things that cannot be seen and touched—such as 'peace' or 'thirst'. Sometimes the picture-writers could get over the difficulty by drawing two or three object-pictures near together or on top of one another. For instance, a wavy line for 'water' and a drawing of a mouth could stand for 'thirst'. But more often they had to represent the idea by means of a symbol—a drawing of something connected with the idea. For instance, a drawing of an ear would come to mean, not only 'ear' itself, but 'hearing', and a bent leg could stand for 'swiftness'.

We still use symbols quite a lot—a cross to represent Christianity; a crown to represent royalty; a dove carrying an olive branch to represent peace. You can think of many more examples for yourself if you try.

The Ancient Egyptians were using picture-writing many thousands of years ago. Egyptian picture-writing is called hieroglyphics, which means sacred writing, or priest writing, because at first the priests, who were the rulers and learned men as well as the religious leaders of the country, were the only people who wrote at all. Object-pictures and idea-pictures and symbols all appear in Egyptian hieroglyphics—and another way of representing words, too.

Have you ever tried to make out a puzzle in which a little story is told in pictures, but each picture stands not for the object represented but for some other word pronounced in the same way? A drawing of a human eye, for instance, may stand for the pronoun I; a rose may represent the past of the verb 'to rise', and a saw the past of 'to see'. We have a great many pairs or groups of words in English which sound the same but have different meanings, and other languages have, too, including the language the Ancient Egyptians spoke. So in hieroglyphics a picture might represent some object, but when the name of the object was spoken, another meaning was intended. A drawing of the skin of an animal, a hide, for instance, might mean 'hide' or 'in' or 'approach', as the same word had all these meanings in the Egyptian language.

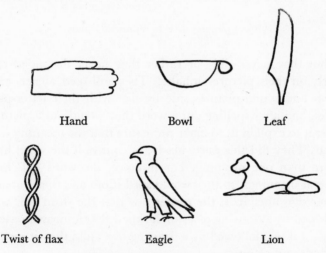

Hand   Bowl   Leaf

Twist of flax   Eagle   Lion

Some signs used in Egyptian hieroglyphics

In time some of the pictures that represented objects began to be used to represent the *sound* of the letter with which the name of the object started. The Egyptian word for water was Nu, and water was represented by a wavy line. Gradually the wavy line came to represent the sound of N. The Egyptian word for mouth was Ro, and the simplified drawing of a mouth came to represent the sound of R. At first many signs

B   17

were used for one letter—there were thirty signs for A alone —but in time the letter signs were simplified until there were twenty-five of them altogether, and the Egyptians had a picture-alphabet with which they could spell out all their words just as we do.

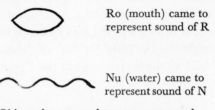

Ro (mouth) came to represent sound of R

Nu (water) came to represent sound of N

Object pictures used to represent sounds

But they never did—or rather they never depended entirely on their picture-alphabet. They still used object- and idea- and sound-pictures side by side with their letter-pictures, and after spelling out a word they would put a picture after it to explain it, to make quite sure that the meaning was clear. They did this particularly, of course, if the word had more than one meaning. For instance, the word 'sef' had several meanings, so they would spell it out and then put another sign after it. If the reader saw that the word 'sef' was followed by a drawing of a sun, he knew that it meant 'yesterday'; if it was followed by a drawing of a child then it meant 'baby', and so on.

A great deal of Egyptian hieroglyphic writing was carved or painted on stone or wood, and it was used to describe or commemorate some important event, or the doings of some great king. There are hieroglyphic inscriptions on the walls of the tombs of some of the very earliest kings of Egypt, who lived between six and seven thousand years ago.

Of course, the Egyptians were not the only people who, starting with pictures, developed a way of writing and a kind of alphabet. All over the world, in China, India, among the primitive peoples of Europe, America and Africa, men learnt to write down their thoughts in many different ways. Several of them produced alphabets of one kind or another. There have been nearly two hundred different alphabets in different parts of the world through the centuries, and about fifty are still in use besides our own.

In Mesopotamia, the district through which the rivers Tigris and Euphrates run, there were highly developed civilizations thousands of years ago, as well as in Egypt. People

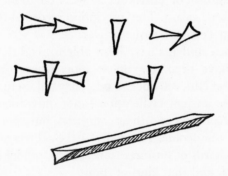

Cuneiform writing and the instrument used in making it

who lived in these areas at different times, such as the Babylonians, the Assyrians, the Hittites, and others, whom we read about in the Bible, developed a way of writing by pressing a kind of pen with a wedge-shaped end into tablets of soft clay. The clay tablets were then baked in an oven, or dried in the sun, until they became hard, like bricks.

We call this kind of writing 'cuneiform', from a Latin word, *cuneus*, meaning a wedge.

The people who wrote in cuneiform made inscriptions on rocks and on buildings as well as on clay tablets. Thousands of years later these inscriptions were noticed and wondered at by travellers, but by that time no one knew what they meant, or even whether they meant anything at all. Then just over a century ago a young British officer named Henry Rawlinson was sent to Persia. He became interested in an inscription that was carved nearly five hundred feet up on the face of a solitary rock at a place called Bihistun in western Persia. He had himself lowered from the top and copied out the inscription, which was in cuneiform and in two other scripts. Rawlinson had studied ancient languages very thoroughly, and after a great deal of hard work he was able to make out what the cuneiform meant. The inscription recorded the triumphs of the great Persian conqueror Darius.

Since then students have been able to read the many tablets that have been dug up at spots where such cities as Babylon and Nineveh once stood. They tell them a great deal about those ancient civilizations—not only about their history and their laws and their conquests, but about the everyday life of the people. For many of the tablets are accounts, receipts, records of business transactions, school lessons, private letters, and that kind of thing.

Archaeologists—the people who excavate the temples, cities, palaces and tombs of the distant past and try to find out all they can about the history of mankind—have found huge collections of baked clay tablets that formed part of big libraries. At a place called Nippur they have found over one hundred thousand. Sometimes the building in which the tablets were kept was destroyed by fire thousands of years ago, but the baked clay tablets were not damaged by the flames, although they have often been broken through falling. Usually the tablets are flat, and the writing is on both sides. A great many tablets were needed to make what we should call one book. The tablets were numbered as we number pages, and a title ran on from one to another.

Sometimes, instead of being done on flat bricks, the writing was done on short clay cylinders, or pipes, which were kept inside an outer case, also of baked clay, on which the title of the book was written. Some of these were dug up when a famous library of Nineveh was excavated. They were probably made about 3000 B.C., so they are the earliest 'book-bindings' we know about.

The tablets and cylinders were sometimes kept in chests and sometimes on shelves round the room. The shelves have generally collapsed and the tablets have been found heaped together on the floor. At Nineveh the floor was over a foot deep in tablets, many broken. They were of different sizes, from the largest which were nine inches by six and a half

A cylinder seal

inches down to the smallest which were only about an inch long, with one or two lines of cuneiform writing so small that it can hardly be read without a magnifying glass.

At one place, called Sippara, the archaeologists were lucky enough to find a library in which the tablets—thousands of them—were resting undisturbed on the shelves, all carefully arranged and numbered just as the librarians left them over three thousand years ago.

We know the name of one librarian of very early times. He worked in the library of Ur, which was the city in which

Abraham grew up and was educated. Perhaps Abraham studied the tablets in this very library. When Ur was being excavated a little clay cylinder was discovered which had belonged to a man named Amil-anu, who is described as tablet-keeper (or librarian) to Emug-sin, King of Babylon. These little clay cylinders were used as seals. They were rolled over soft clay and left an impression of the name and description of the owner.

Many of the libraries, of course, were collections of tablets belonging to kings' palaces—tablets recording what had happened during the reigns of the different kings. Other libraries were attached to temples. The priests made close observations of the sun, moon and stars, so some of their tablets were about astronomy, which is the study of the stars, and astrology, which is the study of the influence which the priests believed that the stars had on man and man's affairs.

In these ancient libraries there were books about agriculture; about building and the best wood and stone to use for it; about law and government; about diseases and medicine; about geography and history. There were grammars and dictionaries, and there were even translations of books written in other countries, or in languages that had been used a thousand years or more earlier, just as we to-day have translations of books written originally n Latin and Greek. There are books, too, about mathematics, and lists of multiplication tables. There are lists of minerals and plants, and at Nineveh a list was found of all the animals then known in Assyria, carefully classified according to species, and with the popular names and the scientific names side by side.

There is poetry, too, and there are stories, such as legends about the creation and the deluge.

Some of the libraries were for the use of the public. Part of the catalogue of a library at a place called Agade is in existence, in which the reader is told to write down his name and particulars about the tablet he wants, when the librarian will take it from the shelves and hand it to him.

You can see some of these clay tablets and cylinders, and the little cylinder seals, in museums such as the British Museum in London.

To us writing by pressing signs into soft clay and then baking the clay hard seems very slow and clumsy. But in Mesopotamia it was the normal way of communicating for generations of people for thousands of years.

But in Egypt a very different kind of material was used for writing purposes from very early times, and a very different kind of writing developed.

CHAPTER II

★

The Ancient Egyptians and their Books

I n Egypt, in the muddy swamps round the delta of the River Nile, there grew a reed called papyrus, of which the stalk was sometimes as much as ten feet high and as thick as a man's arm. From this stalk the Egyptians learnt how to make a kind of paper.

They put thin strips of the papyrus stalk side by side on a flat surface, very close together. Then they wetted them and put another layer of strips over the first, but at right angles, so that the fibres of one layer ran horizontally and of the other vertically. Then they beat or pressed the surface gently until the two layers were stuck firmly together. The sheet was then dried in the sun, and the surface polished by being rubbed with a smooth shell or pebble. The result was a sheet of material something like tough paper, on which people could write or paint.

Pliny, a Roman writer, tells us that the muddy water of the Nile was used to wet the papyrus because it had some special quality that made the two layers stick together, but it is more likely that some kind of gum was mixed with the water.

Sheets of papyrus varied in size. They were often about five to five and a half inches wide by nine to eleven inches long, but those that were to be used for important writings were often sixteen or eighteen inches wide. The sheets were joined together, end to end, to make strips as long as might be necessary for any particular piece of writing, and some very long strips have been found. There is one in the British Museum which is one hundred and thirty-three feet long by sixteen and three-quarter inches wide.

The writing was usually done in columns, rather like the columns in a newspaper, on the side on which the fibres ran horizontally, though sometimes the other side would be used later, perhaps when someone was hard up for a piece of papyrus, and there was no new, clean piece handy. The writing could be washed off with a sponge, and the papyrus used again. When the Egyptians wanted to learn something or they had read something very wise or sacred which they wanted to remember, they would wash the words off the papyrus on which they were written and drink the water.

The scribes wrote with small reeds about ten inches long and only about a sixteenth or an eighteenth of an inch across, and at first the end of the reed was crushed to make it into a kind of brush. Later on the scribes took to using thicker reeds, and to cutting the end into the shape of a pen nib.

They used black ink made from charcoal mixed with water and a little gum, and coloured inks made from mineral earths or, in the case of blue, from a lovely blue stone which we now call lapis lazuli.

When the writing was finished the long strip of papyrus was rolled up and a cord was tied round the middle of it. If the writing was private or important the cord was sealed with a clay seal on which the owner's name or sign was stamped. The rolls were kept in wooden boxes or in earthenware pots.

Papyrus is a fairly tough material and lasts well so long as it does not get damp. The climate of Egypt is dry and the soil is sandy, so immense numbers of papyrus rolls have come down to us in perfect condition, with their ink as black, and their colours as clear, as when they were first written.

The use of papyrus made a great difference to the way in which picture-writing was done. If you like to try a little experiment you will see why this was so. Scratch or carve three or four simple little pictures—say, a bird, a leaf, a tent and a boat—on to a rock or a wall or a piece of wood. Then get a small paint-brush and some ink and copy your four little drawings on to a sheet of paper. Do them fairly slowly and carefully the first time, but afterwards draw or 'write' them again and again, faster and faster, until you are doing them as quickly as though you were writing four familiar letters of

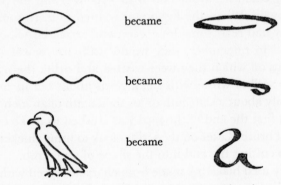

How hieroglyphic writing developed into hieratic

the alphabet. I am pretty certain that you will find that the last drawings, made quickly with a brush, are very different from those scratched on the stone or wood. They probably don't look much like the original objects at all.

Something of this kind happened in Egypt. Hieroglyphics continued to be used all the time for inscriptions on stone and for important writings, but a much freer, simpler style of writing developed through the custom of writing quickly on papyrus with a reed brush or pen. The pictures turned into symbols needing only two or three strokes of the pen. This simpler, quicker kind of writing is called hieratic.

26

The Ancient Egyptians and their Books

We do not know quite when hieratic writing first developed but some papyrus rolls dating from 3500 B.C. that were found in some mummy cases are written in hieratic. This word, like hieroglyphic, means that the writing was done by priests, for at first it was used only for recording sacred books.

Later, hieratic writing was used by all kinds of people for all kinds of purposes. Then, in time, when writing was used for trade, business, education, law and government, and for private letters as well, a third style of writing developed, even simpler than hieratic, which we call demotic.

It is only during the last hundred and fifty years or so that historians have taken much interest in papyri, and a great many rolls must have been discovered and destroyed in the past. The first discovery we know anything about took place in 1778 when some Egyptians who were digging in a part of Egypt called the Fayum found an earthenware pot in which there were about fifty rolls of papyrus. They tried to sell them, but no one was interested, and they fed their fires with all but one. They said that old papyrus rolls smelt nice when they were burning.

The sole surviving roll became the property of an Italian Cardinal named Stefano Borgia. It was not a very old papyrus nor a very exciting one, in comparison with the many that were to be discovered later. It was written in Greek in A.D. 191-2, and was a record of an inspection of the embankment of the River Nile. But the Cardinal had a copy of it printed, so it is interesting because it was the very first Egyptian papyrus ever to be published in Europe, and the very first in which anyone had taken any interest for many hundreds of years.

I expect you know that in 1798 Napoleon's army invaded Egypt. One result of his expedition was that for the first time people became tremendously curious about that ancient land and the marvellous and mysterious things that could be seen there. The native Egyptians found they could make a great deal of money by selling to Europeans any relics of Ancient Egypt they could find, including papyri. So they dug in all likely places, and in particular they searched for the tombs of their ancestors, for in Ancient Egypt all kinds of beautiful and interesting things were buried with the dead. The later Egyptians had discovered that rolls of papyrus had nearly always been placed in the coffins with the bodies (which we call mummies).

Of course, in Napoleon's time no one could read the papyri, so they were bought and kept simply as curiosities. Many of them have probably been destroyed since, or have come to grief through neglect. We know now that the papyri in the tombs are nearly always copies of certain sacred books of Ancient Egypt, usually one called *The Book of the Dead*, or some part of it. The book was meant to tell the dead man or woman things that he must know in order to pass safely through the Underworld, and through the Judgment Hall, and generally to help him to speak and behave properly in the next world. Sometimes the papyrus roll is very long and contains as many as a hundred and fifty chapters; sometimes it is quite short, containing only five or six chapters. The poorest people seem to have had to be content with a scrap of papyrus on which a few words only were written, and this was fastened to the breast of the mummy with gum.

A very large number of scribes must have been employed in Ancient Egypt continuously copying *The Book of the Dead*, and the size and beauty of the copy buried with anyone would depend on how much his relatives could afford to pay.

You can see a very famous and beautiful *Book of the Dead* in the British Museum. It is called the Papyrus of Ani. It is seventy-eight feet long and one foot three inches wide, and it contains sixty-six chapters and many very interesting pictures. Ani seems to have been a scribe, and it is quite possible that he wrote part of his own book himself.

You can see many other interesting papyrus rolls besides the Papyrus of Ani in the British Museum, as well as inscriptions, carved or painted on stone or wood, and they will show you what the three kinds of Egyptian writing—hieroglyphic, hieratic and demotic—were like. You can also see the palettes which the scribes used. They are the shape of rather long pencil-boxes, and are made of wood or ivory, or sometimes alabaster. At one end there are hollows to hold the inks and paints. Down the centre of the rest of the palette

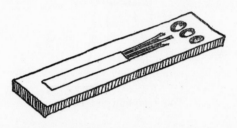

An Egyptian scribe's palette

there is a slot, in which the reed pens or brushes were kept. A sliding cover, or a little crosspiece of wood, kept the reeds in place. Sometimes the palette has the name of the scribe on it, and sometimes a prayer to a god named Thoth, because the Egyptians believed that he had invented the art of writing.

Sometimes there is a picture of Thoth on the palette. He is shown with the body of a man and the head of a bird called an Ibis, and he usually holds a reed pen and a scribe's palette in his hand.

Scribes carried their materials in a kind of satchel with a soft leather top and a leather handle.

Of course, all the papyri found have not been copies of *The Book of the Dead* or other sacred books. Great mounds have been excavated which were the rubbish heaps outside towns of Ancient Egypt, and enormous numbers of papyrus rolls have been found that were thrown away as waste paper

The Egyptian god Thoth

Scribes, as drawn by an Egyptian artist

thousands of years ago. Some are stories, some histories, some records of trials (including the trials of tomb-robbers of nearly three thousand years ago), and a great many are business records and reports. There are many private letters, too. There is one famous letter from a very angry little boy named Theon whose father had gone on a visit to a big city without him. In it Theon declares that if his father does not send for him he won't write or speak to him again, and he will refuse to eat or drink, and will generally make a real nuisance of himself.

There is another well-known letter from a man who had gone away from home to look for work. He writes to his wife telling her that if when her baby is born it is a boy she is to look after it, but if it is a girl she must cast it out to die.

But perhaps you are wondering how anyone to-day can possibly understand anything that is written in the picture-writings of Egypt. That is a thrilling story that we shall come to presently.

CHAPTER III

*

Phœnicians and Greeks

Although papyrus was made in Egypt that was not the only country in which it was used. For centuries the Egyptians manufactured an enormous amount of it, and it was exported to other countries and became the commonest writing material in the ancient world.

For hundreds of years, from about 1200 B.C., the chief traders and merchants of the Mediterranean were people called Phœnicians. They lived along the coast of Syria, and they are the people who in the Bible are called Canaanites. Their chief cities were called Tyre and Sidon.

The Phœnicians had discovered a wonderful dye which they made by collecting an enormous number of the shells of a certain tiny shell-fish and crushing them. The dye was called Tyrian purple, or royal purple, and was tremendously popular, so that the Phœnicians did a great trade in it.

But they traded in all sorts of other things as well, and founded trading stations all round the shores of the Mediterranean, stations which in some cases became great and famous cities, such as Carthage. They even sailed through the straits of Gibraltar and up the coasts of the countries we now call Spain and France, and reached the south-west coast of Britain, where they bought tin.

One of the things the Phœnicians traded in was papyrus

from Egypt. The papyrus was carried by ship from Egypt to an important Phœnician port named Byblos, and from Byblos other ships took it to other countries.

The Phœnicians gave up using clay tablets as their ancestors had done, and learnt how to use the papyrus themselves. They learnt, too, the signs the Egyptians used in their writing. But the Phœnicians were a very business-like people. They wrote mainly in order to make out bills and receipts and records of their trading ventures. They needed a kind of writing that could be written quickly and read easily. So they dropped the picture-signs which the Egyptians had used in addition to their letter-signs, and learned to use the letter-signs only, and to spell out each word just as we do. They were the very first people to depend entirely on an alphabet. Many of their letter-signs developed from those used by the Egyptians, but a few seem to have been taken from some other kind of writing.

The Phœnician alphabet

All the peoples of the ancient world cut inscriptions on stone tablets or rocks in order to record some great historical event or great victory. One of these inscribed stones was found in 1868 near the Dead Sea. It is called the Moabite stone, and it is in the Louvre in Paris. The inscription on it is in Phœnician writing and it is the oldest specimen of such writing that has ever been found. It describes a war that you can read about in the Bible (2 Kings, Chapter 3) between Mesha, King of Moab, and Jehoram, King of Israel. The record was written about 890 B.C., so when it was found the Moabite stone had survived for over two thousand seven hundred years. But soon after its discovery it was very nearly lost for ever. The Arabs, as soon as they found that the Christians were interested in the stone, made up their minds to destroy it. They made the stone very hot and then poured cold water over it, so that it broke into several pieces. Fortunately rubbings had been made earlier, so the stone could be put together again.

One of the countries to which Phœnician ships carried the papyrus they had bought from the Egyptians was Ancient Greece. The Greeks called the papyrus by the name of the Phœnician port from which it had come—Byblos. This was

PHOENICIAN   EARLY GREEK

aleph (ox) △ or ⋈   △ alpha

daleth (door) △   △ delta

nun (fish) ⌐ or ⅄   ∧ nu

How the Greeks changed some of the Phœnician letters

not a very unusual thing to do. Foreign objects and materials are often called by the name of the town or country they have come from. We still call fine porcelain 'china' because the first porcelain cups and bowls came to us from China, and stout linen cloth is called 'holland' because Holland is the country from which we first imported it. You can probably think of several other examples.

The word byblos which the Greeks used for papyrus came in time to mean a book, and centuries later, in Christian times, the word meant, to the Christians, the most important book of all, the Scriptures. So the word has come down to us as the Bible.

The Greeks not only bought papyrus from the Phœnicians, but they adopted their way of writing and their alphabet. But the Phœnician alphabet was all consonants, and although the language the Phœnicians spoke could be written clearly without vowels, Greek could not. So as time went on the Greeks changed some of the Phœnician consonant signs which they did not need into vowels, and added other signs.

But for a long time the forms of the letters were not fixed so that everyone wrote them in the same way, or even used exactly the same letters. And words were not even written always in the same direction. When we write nowadays we always start on the left-hand side of the page. But in the ancient world people wrote from left to right or from right to left, or even from top to bottom of the page, just as it suited them. The Greeks even wrote sometimes in both directions, with one line going from left to right with the letters facing one way, and the next line going from right to left with the letters reversed. This kind of writing was called 'boustrophedon', which means that it was done in the same way in which a team of oxen plough a field—backwards and forwards.

WRITINGDONETHISWAYISCALLEDBOUSTRO
PHEDONBECAUSEOXENPLOUGHINGAFIEL
DWENTTOANDFROINTHESAMEWAY

Boustrophedon writing

We should find it very confusing if our writing was done this way, especially as in the writing of Ancient Greece, and of other countries of the ancient world, there were no spaces between the words, and no paragraphs, and no commas or full stops or other punctuation marks. Here are a few lines of English written in capital letters, backwards and forwards across the page, without any gaps between the words, so that

35

you can see what this kind of writing looks like, and how confusing it is to read.

By the sixth century B.C. the Greeks had decided that writing from left to right was the most convenient, and by the
fifth century B.C. they had decided on the form and number
of the letters of their alphabet. The Greek alphabet of twenty-
four letters was officially accepted by Athens in 403 B.C. and
soon spread all over Greece, and wherever Greek-speaking
people were found.

A B Γ Δ E Z H Θ I K Λ M N Ξ O Π
P Σ T Y Φ X Ψ Ω

The official Greek alphabet

There are Greek statues from this time, and even earlier,
showing people holding papyrus rolls, or sitting with open
rolls in their hands, reading.

The Phœnicians called the letters of their alphabet by the
names of the objects which they had originally represented—
aleph (ox); beth (house); gimel (camel); daleth (door); and
so on. The Greeks adopted the same names, changing them
slightly, so that they became alpha, beta, gamma, delta, etc.
The word 'alphabet' comes from the names of the first two
letters of the Greek alphabet, alpha and beta.

During the fourth century B.C. the Greeks became the
leaders of the world in thought, in art, and in literature, and
Athens became a great centre of learning and discussion.
Then, in the third century B.C., Alexander the Great de-
feated the Persians and made himself master of the great
Persian Empire, and of the lands bordering the eastern Mediterranean, including Egypt.

Alexander destroyed Tyre and Sidon, the two great
Phœnician trading ports, and founded a new city in Egypt
to take their place. It was called Alexandria, and became

tremendously important and prosperous. When Alexander died in 323 B.C., one of his generals, who was named Ptolemy, became King of Egypt.

Ptolemy and the members of his court spoke Greek, of course, and for some centuries Greek was the official language of Egypt. You may remember that the fifty papyrus rolls mentioned in Chapter II, that were found in 1778, dated from the second century A.D., and were written in Greek.

Ptolemy was very enthusiastic about learning and about helping others to learn all they possibly could. So he founded a kind of college at Alexandria which was called the Museum, because it was dedicated to the nine goddesses who, the Greeks believed, presided over the arts and sciences, and who were called the Muses. The Museum at Alexandria became a very famous centre for study and for the investigation of all kinds of problems. Alexandria rivalled Athens itself in importance.

As well as the Museum, Ptolemy founded a great library at Alexandria, which was very famous indeed. It contained copies of all the books written by the great Greek writers, but although the library was in Egypt, there were no Egyptian books in it at all. The library was in two parts, one part being in Ptolemy's palace and the other in a temple called the Temple of Serapis.

If only this wonderful library had survived we should know a great deal more about Greek literature than we do. But the Romans, under Julius Caesar, captured Alexandria in 47 B.C. and a large part of the library was burnt. Then, in A.D. 291, the Christians destroyed the Temple of Serapis and all the treasures that it contained. The same kind of tragedy occurred everywhere in time, and fine collections of books in private and public libraries were destroyed, so that only a few of the books that were written by the great writers of Ancient Greece have survived.

The library at Alexandria kept a staff of men busy all the time copying books, and many of the Greeks and Greek-speaking people who lived in Egypt at this time had books of their own, just as we do. By 'books' we still, of course, mean papyrus rolls. As you read in Chapter II, the dry air and sandy soil of Egypt make it possible for buried and hidden papyrus rolls to exist undamaged for thousands of years, which is not the case anywhere else. So papyrus rolls, or fragments of them, are constantly being dug up in Egypt, and there is always a chance that some of the lost masterpieces of Greece may be found.

The most popular books among Greeks and Greek-speaking people seem to have been the *Odyssey* and the *Iliad*, particularly the *Iliad*, by the great Greek poet Homer. These books had, of course, been written originally hundreds of years earlier, but Greeks still read them and liked to possess copies, just as many of us have copies of the works of Chaucer, Shakespeare, Milton, and other writers of the past.

CHAPTER IV

★

The Rosetta Stone

One of the most valuable and interesting things dating from the time of the Ancient Greeks that has been found in Egypt is not a papyrus roll, but a stone. It was found in 1799 by a young French officer named Bouchard, who was in Egypt with Napoleon's army. The town near which it was found was called Rashid, but Europeans call it Rosetta, so this famous stone is called the Rosetta Stone. Bouchard noticed that there were inscriptions on the stone in three different scripts, the top one being in the hieroglyphics of ancient Egypt, and the bottom one in Greek.

Bouchard guessed that the three inscriptions might be three versions of the same text, and that, as one was in Greek and so could be read, it might be a great help in deciphering the other two. The stone was sent to Cairo, and Napoleon himself, as well as some learned men who had gone to Egypt with him, took a great interest in it. Napoleon had ink impressions made from the stone and sent to scholars all over Europe.

In 1802, after the defeat of Napoleon, the Rosetta Stone was taken to London, and anyone who likes can see it in the British Museum.

The Greek part of the inscription was soon deciphered. It

was found to be a copy of a decree passed by a General Council of Egyptian priests who met at Memphis in 196 B.C. It says how grateful they are to Ptolemy V, who was then King of Egypt, for a number of good things he had done for the country, such as reducing certain taxes, making gifts to temples, releasing prisoners, rebuilding sacred buildings, and so on. In return the priests said they were going to set up statues to Ptolemy in all temples, were going to make his birthday and coronation day festivals for ever, were going to hold special services in his honour, and do many other things of the same kind.

The deciphering of the first inscription, in hieroglyphics, and of the second, which was in demotic—the popular, shortened form of writing which the Egyptians had developed—took far longer. A start was made by an Englishman, Thomas Young. In hieroglyphic writing certain groups of signs are enclosed in an oval space, and Young discovered that these ovals, or 'cartouches' as we call them, always contain a royal name. But the greater part of the work of deciphering the Rosetta Stone was done by a Frenchman, Jean François Champollion.

There is only one cartouche in the hieroglyphic inscription on the Rosetta Stone. So it was clear that if the hieroglyphic inscription was the same as the Greek, then the name must be Ptolemy.

On an obelisk which Young, Champollion and others had examined at a place called Philae there were also two inscriptions, one in Greek and one in hieroglyphics, and in the Greek part two royal names were mentioned, Ptolemy (another Ptolemy, who lived about two hundred years after the one on the Rosetta Stone) and Cleopatra. There were two cartouches in the hieroglyphic section, and one of them was the same as the one on the Rosetta Stone—so it seemed fairly certain that this cartouche stood for Ptolemy. The two cartouches are like this (only the other way round because hieroglyphics are written from right to left):

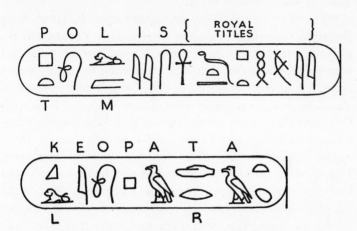

The cartouches of Ptolemy and Cleopatra

You can see that some of the letters in the two names are the same, and so are some of the hieroglyphic signs. By replacing the signs with letters, and then filling in the rest of the letters in the name Cleopatra (with a K at the beginning for the hard sound of C) the early decipherers already had the meaning of eight signs. They found, too, that in some cartouches containing Cleopatra's name the seventh sign, the hand, was sometimes replaced by the little dome-shaped sign that is the second sign in the Ptolemy cartouche, so both signs must stand for the sound of T. They were still left with the two little signs at the end of Cleopatra's cartouche.

You remember, don't you, that the Egyptians never depended entirely on an alphabet, or even on sound-pictures. Thomas Young, Champollion, and other students who were trying to read the Rosetta Stone, noticed that the same two little signs always appeared at the end of the name of a goddess or queen, so they assumed that they meant that the name that came before them was the name of a woman, and that she was divine or royal.

When the name Ptolemy was spelt out, in its Greek form Ptolemaios (spelt Ptolmis, they discovered, in Egyptian hieroglyphics), there were quite a number of signs left over, and Champollion assumed that they must stand for a phrase that appeared in the Greek inscription, 'ever-living, beloved of Ptah'. But it was only after years of hard work that Champollion was able to work out the meaning of these and the many other signs in Egyptian hieroglyphics. Working out the royal names was only a beginning, though a very important one. Champollion was able to go ahead and learn how to read hieroglyphics because he already knew Coptic, which was the language the early Christian descendants of the Ancient Egyptians used. The Scriptures had been translated into Coptic from Greek in the early days of Christianity, and the Coptic language had not been forgotten because these translations still existed, not written in hieroglyphics, of course, but in the Greek alphabet.

Ptolemy V, whose name appears on the Rosetta Stone, did something that, in time, was to have an important effect on writing everywhere, though he did not know it. At a city called Pergamos a library had been formed that looked as though it might become a rival to the one at Alexandria. Ptolemy, we are told, gave orders that the export of papyrus from Egypt to Pergamos was to cease. He knew that, in his day and in his part of the world, books could not be produced without papyrus, any more than we nowadays can produce them without paper. But Eumenes, King of Pergamos, was not to be beaten. He gave orders that something to take the place of papyrus must be found.

Other materials, such as bark, boards, linen and leather had been used in different places from time to time for writing purposes. Perhaps the most satisfactory was leather, because it could be rolled and did not wear out quickly. We know that the Hebrews had their copies of the law and of the Scriptures written on skins. So it was to skins that the people of Pergamos turned when they could not get papyrus. But they did not treat the skins as they would if they were making leather. First they washed the skins thoroughly, then they scraped them perfectly clean on both sides, stretched and dried them, rubbed them with pumice to make them really smooth, and then dressed them with chalk. In the end they had a beautiful smooth surface, almost white, and perfect for writing on. Skin prepared in this way was called by the Romans, some centuries later, pergamena, because they believed that it was first made in Pergamos, and it is known to us as parchment, or vellum.

Strictly speaking, the word vellum should only be used if the skin is that of a calf, but actually it is used for parchment of fine quality whether it is made from calf, sheep, kid, goat, ass, or any other skin.

Some people believe that parchment was known before the time of Ptolemy V and Eumenes, and that the people of Pergamos did not actually discover how to make it, but only that they were the first people to use it for books, and then only when they could not get papyrus. They probably improved it very much and made better parchment than ever before.

About two hundred years later, after part of the library at Alexandria had been burnt, the Roman general, Marc Antony, presented two hundred thousand books from the library at Pergamos to Cleopatra, Queen of Egypt, in order to make good the loss. How it would have grieved Eumenes to see his precious books being sent away to the rival library at Alexandria. But both libraries were to disappear in time. The one at Pergamos has been traced and the ruins excavated, but of the famous library at Alexandria, not a trace remains.

Although the people of Pergamos, according to the story, used parchment some time near the beginning of the second century B.C., it did not become really popular as a writing material and did not begin to take the place of papyrus until nearly five hundred years later. For books papyrus seems to have been regarded as the only possible material.

When people in Ancient Greece and Rome wanted to write something that need not be kept for a long time, they

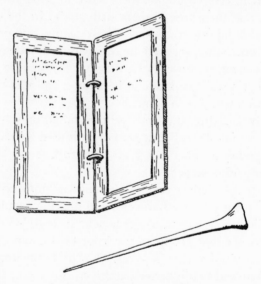

Waxed tablets and a stylus

used neither papyrus nor parchment, but something quite different. Every educated man or woman had his or her set of wax tablets. The tablets were of wood and were like little trays with raised edges. The centre part was coated with wax, and the tablets were used as we use note-books, or exercise-books in school. The writing was scratched on the wax with a pointed instrument called a stylus, and corrections could be made by scratching a little of the wax away with the other end of the stylus, which was flattened and blunt, or by slightly melting the wax and then re-hardening it.

Letters could be written on wax tablets, and if necessary two or three could be put together and a cord tied round them and sealed, so that the letter would only be read by the person it was intended for. After he had read the letter he could melt it away and write his answer on the re-hardened wax.

Often the tablets had holes down one edge and two or three would be fastened together by means of leather laces, rather in the form of a modern book. Such a set of tablets was called a codex, from a Latin word meaning a block of wood, or a board. A codex with two tablets was a diptych, with three a triptych, and so on.

In the British Museum there is a wax tablet with a piece of the original lace still filling up one of the holes, and there is another in existence with the Greek alphabet scratched on the wooden border. One can imagine a little Greek girl or boy learning the alphabet by carefully copying the letters on to the wax.

CHAPTER V

The Romans and their Books

The Romans adopted the alphabet from the Greeks about 700 B.C. They added some letters and dropped or altered others, and gradually worked out the alphabet that we ourselves use, except that the fully developed Roman alphabet had twenty-three letters, and ours has twenty-six. The Roman alphabet had no U, W or J.

GREEK	EARLY LATIN
Β	B
⟨	C
▷	D
Λ	L
Ѕ	S

How the Romans changed some of the Greek letters

The Romans settled the form and order of the letters, and they made them more beautiful than they had ever been before. To them an inscription on a building was not just something to be read; it was a beautiful thing, an ornament, in it-self. They were very particular about the proportions of the letters—that the height should be correct for the width in each case, and that the two parts of letters such as B and R should balance each other properly.

Through the Romans the alphabet and their way of form-ing the letters spread to all the countries they conquered, in-cluding Britain.

The way they wrote figures also spread over Europe and was used for over a thousand years. The first four figures were upright strokes representing one, two, three or four fingers. The V for five represented the hand held up with all the fingers close together and the thumb separated. VI represented the hand plus one, and so on. The X for ten was equal to two V's—or two hands. Later they came to write a figure such as nine by putting the stroke for one in front of the X for ten, meaning ten *minus* one. Larger numbers such as one hundred were indicated by writing the first letter of the word used for hundred—C for centum.

Serifs

When carving an inscription on a building the Romans, for the first time, made the different strokes of the letters different widths. The horizontal strokes were made thinner than the perpendicular, and strokes such as the first in A and the first and third in M and N were thinner than the others. The curves in letters like O and C were made full and big, and the line broadened at the roundest part of the letter.

The Romans noticed that, when cut on a building, straight perpendicular strokes such as I and L, seen from a little distance, tended to look thinner at the ends than in the middle, so they made up for it by thickening the ends. These thickened ends became an essential part of the letters and are called 'serifs'.

Another thing they noticed was that when an inscription was high up the letters in the first line tended to look smaller

Trajan's Column

than those in the last. So they made the letters in the first line slightly larger than those in the second, the second larger than the third, the third than the fourth and so on.

There is a very famous inscription in Rome that is known all over the world, wherever the Roman alphabet is used. Its letters are so clear and beautiful that it has been a model for eighteen hundred years. It is on a great column which is called Trajan's Column, because it was erected in A.D. 114, in the days of the Emperor Trajan. Trajan wanted to make a big new forum (the market-place of a Roman city) in Rome and in order to do it he had a hill levelled. The column shows how high the hill was. All the way up it are sculptures which tell the story of Trajan's victories over some people called Dacians, and the inscription is on the pedestal, ten feet above the ground.

But fine though the Trajan inscription is, another was discovered in 1924 that many people consider even more beautiful, because the letters are lighter looking and more graceful, and they are beautifully grouped, or arranged. This new inscription was found in England. It was put up in A.D. 130 over the main gateway of the forum in the Roman city of Uriconium, which is now Wroxeter in Shropshire. It was in honour of the Emperor Hadrian, who had the great wall built across the north of England which we call Hadrian's Wall. Hadrian came to England himself, and it is possible that he may have visited Uriconium.

The forum was destroyed by fire in A.D. 280 and the inscribed tablet came crashing down seventeen feet to the ground, where it smashed to pieces and was buried under ruins, rubbish and earth. It lay there completely hidden and forgotten for over sixteen hundred years, until Professor Donald Atkinson found a hundred and sixty-nine of the pieces and had them put together again. The inscription was not complete, but there was enough to show what a very beautiful piece of lettering it had been.

You can see casts of the Trajan inscription and of the Hadrian inscription in the Victoria and Albert Museum in London, and in the Museum of the Manchester College of Art—and probably in other museums, too.

The Romans and their Books

The Romans conquered the Greeks in the second century B.C. and after that large numbers of Greek works of art flowed to Rome as well as many Greek books and Greek booksellers and scribes. There was a tremendous demand for books, for the Romans wanted to learn all they could of Greek thought and learning.

They also wrote books themselves, of course. When a man had written a book many copies of it had to be made, so that people could buy and read it. People who have copies of an author's book made and distribute the copies to the booksellers, are now called publishers. There were publishers in Ancient Rome. All books had to be copied by hand, so the publishers had to have a large staff of scribes.

The scribes were slaves, and many of them were Greeks. We are told that a well-educated slave who knew Greek was very expensive—about £1000 in our money. Sometimes slaves were trained from childhood to be scribes.

We think the work to be copied was probably dictated. As the slaves had cost so much money, their owners would want them to produce as many books as possible. The slave copyists probably had to work rapidly, and perhaps for long hours. Three or four hundred copies of a book would be produced in a few days. Anyway, it is certain that the scribes made a great many mistakes. Sometimes publishers employed special scribes to look through the books and correct them. Roman writers were always complaining about the carelessness with which books were copied. When the books were in Latin the trouble may have been due to the copyists being Greeks and not knowing Latin very well.

The first letters of books, or of sections of books, were written in red. The red paint was called minium, and the man who applied it to the book was called the miniator. From this word we get our word 'miniature', meaning a little picture painted on ivory or some similar material, although the miniator of Ancient Rome had nothing to do with pictures, but only with writing.

The very first publisher whose name is known to us was called Atticus. He was a friend of Cicero's, and published his books. We are told that he was very wealthy and owned many highly educated slaves and copyists. Some of the letters that Cicero wrote to Atticus are in existence. In one Cicero forbids Atticus to sell uncorrected copies of one of his books, and in another he asks Atticus to have a mistake that he, Cicero, had made, corrected before the books were sent out.

Boy reading from a roll

Of course, when we speak of books in Ancient Rome we still mean papyrus rolls. Anyone reading a book held the papyrus roll with both hands. It was unrolled by the right hand and rolled up again as it was read by the left hand. When the whole roll had been read it had to be rolled back again so that it was ready for the next reader. Generally a rod of wood, ebony, ivory, or even, occasionally, gold, was put inside the roll or attached to the end of the piece of papyrus for it to be wound round. Our word 'volume' really means something that is revolved—a roll, or scroll.

The rolls were kept on shelves, with labels, sometimes of parchment, hanging out, on which the titles of the books were written. Books of any length would cover several rolls. Homer's *Iliad* or *Odyssey*, which perhaps you can have a chance of seeing in modern book-form, took up at least twenty-four rolls of papyrus each.

Whole cargoes of papyrus were shipped to Rome from Egypt. It came in rolls of various sizes and widths and qualities ready for use, the different grades being known by names such as Imperial and Royal. For scientific works writers liked large sheets of papyrus, but for poetry smaller sheets were preferred.

Papyrus rolls did not last so well in any other country as they did in Egypt. In Rome a book two hundred years old was considered rather exceptional. The constant rolling and unrolling wore them badly, and we are told that moth did them a great deal of damage. Sometimes papyrus rolls were kept inside covers of purple leather and were tied with a scarlet cord.

The Romans, like the Greeks, had collections of books, or private libraries, of their own. Julius Caesar planned to set up a public library in Rome, but he was killed before he could do it, so Rome's first public library was founded by a man named Asinius Pollio in 39 B.C. It was the first public library in the world to contain books (papyrus rolls, of course) written in Latin as well as in Greek.

Other libraries were founded as time went on, so that by the year A.D. 350 there were twenty-eight public libraries in Rome. The ruins of some of them have been excavated, so that we know where they stood, but not a fragment of the many thousands of papyrus rolls they contained has survived.

Unlike the baked clay books of Mesopotamia, the papyrus rolls of Rome could not withstand fire, damp and neglect.

The only place outside Egypt where papyrus rolls have been found is Herculaneum. The cities of Pompeii and Herculaneum were buried in lava during an eruption of the volcano Vesuvius in 79 A.D. For nearly seventeen hundred years the two towns lay undisturbed, just as they had been left by the terrified inhabitants. Then, in 1754, the excavation of Herculaneum began.

For anyone interested in books and their history one of the most exciting things discovered in Herculaneum was a room about twelve feet square in one of the villas. It had been the library of the house. All round the walls were the remains of bookcases and, more exciting still, the charred remains of hundreds of rolls of papyrus. In the centre of the room was a table, at which the reader could sit while studying his books. An extraordinary thing is that although the rolls were so charred it has been found possible to unroll and read some of them. They are all books of one kind—books on philosophy—and date from about the first century B.C.

On some of the walls of Pompeii paintings have survived. Two of them show young girls standing with open papyrus rolls in their hands, reading. Another is a portrait of a man and a woman. The man is holding a closed roll in his hand and the woman has a pair of waxed tablets and a stylus. A wall painting at Herculaneum is a 'still-life' group, showing materials used in writing, such as a roll of papyrus, an ink-well, a reed pen, and a set of waxed tablets.

CHAPTER VI

★

The Book Changes its Shape

To our way of thinking the roll form of book is very inconvenient, and it seems a most surprising thing that people should have gone on using it, as they did, for thousands of years.

In other ways reading was not made easy in ancient times. Written work was not divided into chapters, or even into paragraphs, and there was hardly any punctuation. The title of the book and the name of the author often did not appear on the roll at all (except on the label that hung from it), but if it did it was usually at the end of the roll, not at the beginning.

Nowadays if we want people to read something from a certain book we can give them the page number, or can at least tell them which chapter the statement is in. But when books were in the form of rolls one could only give the name of the book and its author, and the whole roll had to be opened and read until the passage referred to was found.

In spite of all these disadvantages it was not until early Christian times that a different way of making a book began to be practised.

The new way was to take sheets of a writing material, fold them, and stitch them together at the folds, so producing the kind of book we know to-day. An ancient book written by hand but made up in pages like a modern book, instead of being in the form of a roll, was called by the same name as the sets of wooden tablets—a codex. The plural is codices.

At one time it was thought that the codex form of book was not used until after people had given up using papyrus and taken to using parchment instead, but a few years ago some ancient manuscripts (that means hand-written books) were discovered which showed that this was not the case. Twelve manuscripts were found by some Egyptians, no one knows quite how or where. Some say that they were in jars, buried under the ruins of a very ancient building; others say that the jars were found in an old Coptic graveyard. Whatever the truth may have been, the manuscripts found their way into the hands of dealers who sold most of them to an American gentleman living in England, a Mr. A. Chester-Beatty, so they are called the Chester-Beatty papyri.

The discovery made a very great stir for two reasons. One was that although the manuscripts were written on papyrus they were all codices; and the other was that they were all parts of the Bible written in Greek, and some of them were the oldest copies of any part of the Bible that had ever been found.

The Bible, which we now know as one book, is really a collection of a large number of books, all written at different times and places and by different people. The Old Testament contains the scriptures or sacred books of the Jews, whose home was in Palestine. They were originally written during the eight hundred or so years before Christ, and in the language of the Jews, which was Hebrew. The New Testament contains books written about Jesus and his disciples and followers, and epistles (which means letters) written by St. Paul and other apostles to little Christian communities in various places during the three hundred or so years after Jesus's death, when Christians were being persecuted. They were originally written in Greek, because that was the language spoken by most of the peoples living in the countries bordering the eastern end of the Mediterranean at that time.

All these different books were, of course, originally written by hand and were copied and re-copied century after century, as they were wanted. But the copyists did not always copy accurately. Sometimes they made mistakes, and sometimes they deliberately left out something which they thought might be wrong or unnecessary, or added a bit of their own. So when very ancient copies of any books of the Bible are found it is very seldom that any two ever agree exactly. The earlier a copy is the nearer it is likely to be to the original book.

Until very recently we had no very early copies of any of the books of the Old Testament in the language in which they were originally written—Hebrew. One reason is this. In A.D. 70 Jerusalem was destroyed and the Jews lost their country and were scattered. They clung to their religion and to their scriptures, and they decided that it was necessary that they should make up their minds exactly which of their ancient books really were sacred, and should settle exactly what was the correct wording of each book. So about the year A.D. 100 a kind of conference, called a Synod, of Jews made a list of the sacred books. They are the books we find in our Old Testament to-day. The Synod left out certain other Hebrew writings which they decided were not really sacred. We can read them in a book called the Apocrypha.

The Synod decided exactly what the wording of the sacred texts should be, and ordered that any copies found incorrect or damaged were to be replaced by accurate copies and the old copies were to be destroyed.

Until a very short time ago the oldest copies of any of the Old Testament books in Hebrew which were known to exist were no earlier than the ninth and tenth centuries A.D. But the Jewish scribes had such a respect for their sacred writings and were so careful in their copying during the eight hundred years after the Synod met, that the Old Testament books are believed to have come down to us almost exactly in the form which the Synod authorized.

Scholars, naturally, would like to know what the Hebrew Scriptures were like before the Synod met, and how they differed from the version the Synod agreed upon. But apparently none has survived. So you can imagine how thrilled they were when, in 1949, the fact came to light that about two years before some very early Hebrew manuscripts had been found in a cave in Palestine. A shepherd searching for one of his goats among the rocky hills near the Dead Sea had come upon a hole in a rock and had thrown a stone through it. To his surprise he heard something that sounded like earthenware breaking. Later he and a companion wriggled through the hole, and in the cavern beyond found some large jars, one broken by the stone, and fragments of several others. Inside the jars they found eight leather scrolls covered with strange writing.

The shepherds took four scrolls each and sold them to dealers in Bethlehem. In time some of the scrolls found their way to a university and some to a monastery in Jerusalem, while some reached America. Experts set to work to examine and photograph them.

Later the cave itself was carefully excavated and examined, and remains of about forty jars were discovered and hundreds of fragments of Old Testament manuscripts. Experts were able to decide that the jars, which must originally have contained about two hundred scrolls, were hidden in the cave some time during the second century B.C., and that they had been disturbed in Roman times—probably some time early in the third century A.D. Two Roman lamps and a cooking pot were discovered.

One of the leather scrolls was a complete copy of the Book of Isaiah. It was in an almost perfect state of preservation and was about twenty-two feet long. The other scrolls, and the fragments, contained parts of the Books of Genesis, Deuteronomy, Leviticus, Judges, Daniel and others. They were written during the second, third and fourth centuries before Christ, so that they are more than a thousand years older than any other Old Testament books in Hebrew previously known to exist.

Before these leather scrolls were discovered the earliest copies of the Old Testament we had were written, not in the original Hebrew, but in Greek. Long before the destruction of Jerusalem in A.D. 70 the Jews had begun to spread over all the countries bordering the Mediterranean. So in the third century before Christ (about three hundred and fifty years before the Synod met) it was considered necessary to translate the Hebrew Scriptures into Greek for the benefit of the Jews who spoke only Greek, and no longer used Hebrew as their language. The work of translating was done in Alexandria, where at this time, you remember, the first Ptolemys were busy founding the great library and museum. Seventy-two men are said to have worked on the translation, so this first Greek Old Testament is called the Septuagint, which means the 'work of the seventy'.

As the Septuagint was made before the Synod of A.D. 100 it contains the books that were banned by the Synod, the books that appear in the Apocrypha.

The Chester-Beatty papyri which were found in Egypt were copies of the Septuagint, and of certain books of the New Testament. Some of them are believed to date from the second century A.D. The fact that they are codices and that fragments of other Christian books which were evidently codices have also been found from time to time, shows that this kind of book was made and used by the early Christians long before codices took the place of rolls in Rome and over the rest of the Roman Empire.

One reason why the Christians took to making their books in this way may have been that the new churches all wanted copies of the various books of the Bible, both of the Old and the New Testament, and if they had them all they had to have an enormous number of papyrus rolls. A roll could not be made very long or it would be too thick when rolled up to be held comfortably and would be unmanageable. So only one book of the Bible could go on one roll. But in a codex several books could be combined. In the Chester-Beatty papyri the four Gospels, Matthew, Mark, Luke and John, and the Acts of the Apostles are all together in one codex, and nearly all the Epistles of St. Paul are in another. And the earliest codex of them all, which is believed to have been written between A.D. 120 and A.D. 150, contains the two books Numbers and Deuteronomy, while another contains the books of Ezekiel, Daniel and Esther.

Perhaps another reason why the early Christians seem often to have used the codex rather than the roll was that in a codex it was far easier to turn up any particular passage that was wanted than it was in a roll.

During the first three centuries after the death of Christ the Christians were often persecuted and their churches and their books were burnt. So hundreds of these early copies of the Bible, or parts of it, both rolls and codices, must have been lost.

The Christians were not the only people who had their books destroyed. Some of the Roman emperors gave orders for large numbers of books to be burnt if they did not happen to like or approve of them, and some of the more tyrannical emperors, such as Tiberius and Domitian, had the authors, publishers, and even the copyists killed as well.

Although the Christians seem to have used papyrus codices

quite early, the papyrus roll continued to be the usual type of book in Ancient Rome until the fourth century A.D. Then, gradually, parchment or vellum began to take the place of papyrus and the codex of the roll.

A Roman writer named Martial who lived from A.D. 40 until A.D. 104 is the first to mention books (meaning rolls) written on parchment, but he seems to be referring to note-books, and to books of little extracts from great writers and poets, which were intended as presents. Sometimes during the next two centuries parchment seems to have been used, too, for school books, records, legal books and so on, which had to be referred to again and again, and which would have very hard wear. Then people began to realize that it was easier to cut the parchment into sheets, fold them and stitch them together, so making codices, than to fasten them together end to end and so make rather heavy, clumsy rolls.

But such books were looked upon as very inferior to the papyrus rolls. A Roman lawyer named Ulpian, who died in A.D. 229, even discussed whether, when a library was left to someone by a man who had died, the parchment codices in it were to be regarded as books at all!

Early in the fourth century the parchment codex did at last become popular, and before long parchment had almost entirely taken the place of papyrus and had become the accepted material from which books were to be made for the next thousand years. But even so, the use of papyrus for some purposes dragged on for centuries. Even as late as 1022 the Pope was issuing his 'Bulls', as the Pope's announcements are called, on papyrus.

The task of rewriting all the literature of Ancient Greece and Rome on parchment and in codex form began during the fourth century. An edict by the Emperor Valentinian in A.D. 372 mentions staffs of copyists being employed at libraries to produce codices.

Some of the new books seem to have been very elaborate. The mother of an emperor named Maximinius, when he was young, gave him a copy of the work of Homer written on purple vellum in golden ink. Vellum was often tinted with saffron and other colours. Purple would only be used for books intended for people of the highest rank. Often if the writing was to be in gold the vellum was tinted crimson; if in silver, it was tinted a bluish colour. The Emperor Nero had some verses of his own written in gold.

You remember that three thousand or more years before the Trajan and Hadrian inscriptions were written, or the Roman Empire even existed, the priests in Egypt, in writing

ETQVANDOINEIDVMREM

Square capitals

QuIDSYRIISAUTSCYLLAMHIQ·

Rustic capitals

their hieroglyphics rapidly on papyrus, developed a quicker, more free way of writing the signs. The same kind of thing happened among the scribes of Rome. In the first 'book-hand' that developed, the letters—all in capitals, of course—were similar to the letters carved on the inscriptions. The downstrokes in such letters as N and M were thick and the upstrokes thin, and the round letters were complete circles or parts of circles. There were serifs at the ends of the straight strokes. Manuscripts in which the letters are formed in this way are said to be written in 'square capitals'.

Soon another way of writing the letters developed, in which the writing is said to be in 'rustic capitals'. Rustic capitals are pushed up together more closely than square capitals, and the round letters are no longer full circles. Some lines which are straight in the square capitals are slightly curved in the rustic—in fact, the V has become more like a U.

In both these ways of writing the capital letters were all written quite separately, without any connection between them. As a rule there was no space between the words either.

While books and other important documents were being written in these rather severe formal letters, the ordinary men and women who were writing to each other on their sheets of papyrus or their waxed tablets, were using a much freer kind of writing. They tended to keep the pen down on the surface on which they were writing—to 'run on' from letter to letter. So this kind of informal writing is called 'cursive' or 'running'.

NumquidNONiamsciebamsqui

Uncial writing

In time the informal cursive handwriting began to have some influence on the book hands, and a kind of writing developed which we call 'Uncial'. Some people say that the word uncial comes from the Latin word uncia, which means an inch and indicates that the letters were usually about an inch high. Others say it comes from the Latin word uncus which means crooked. In any case, we use the term to describe a certain kind of writing, to distinguish it both from the square and the rustic capitals.

Uncials were still capital letters, though the strokes of some letters were taken above or below the lines. But the greatest difference between uncials and the other book-hands is that some of the strokes that were straight in the other hands were rounded in the uncials. The letters A, D, E and M, for instance, were written something like this:

$$\text{a} \quad \text{∂} \quad \text{ε} \quad \text{m}$$

The serifs became just a flick of the pen, or were dropped altogether.

During the fourth century, when the parchment codex was taking the place of the papyrus roll, two very important things happened. One was that the Roman Empire accepted Christianity and in A.D. 327 the Emperor Constantine was baptized; and the other was that in A.D. 330 Constantine founded a new capital for the eastern, Greek-speaking, half of the Roman Empire at Byzantium, and renamed it Constantinople.

Greek scholars and book-lovers gathered round Constantine in his new capital, and he ordered that a search should be made for Christian books—not so that they could be destroyed as had often happened in the past, but so that they could be preserved. By the time he died seven years later he had a collection of about seven thousand books. His descendants added to the collection until the library became very big indeed.

All over the Roman Empire there must have been people asking for copies of the Bible, and they would have wanted it complete. So for the first time parchment books in codex form were produced that contained the whole of the Old and the New Testaments in one volume. We know that Constantine ordered fifty copies of the Bible in Greek to be written on vellum for his new capital.

Some of the Christian books produced both in Rome and in Constantinople were as elaborate as the pagan codices, being written in gold and silver inks on tinted vellum. Many churchmen did not like such books. They said they were a sinful extravagance, but they continued to be made. Very few exist now, but there is a copy of part of the Gospels written in silver on purple vellum at a place called Upsala in Sweden. It is called the Codex Argentues, or silver book.

As time passed nearly all the early copies of the Bible in Greek disappeared, just as so many other books of the Ancient world did. Sometimes as the centuries passed a Bible would become old and worn out and would be replaced by a new copy; sometimes when new ways of writing had developed which I shall be telling you about presently, the huge old books may have been considered old-fashioned and have been discarded in favour of newer-looking books. But even more often they were destroyed by the rough barbarians who swarmed over the western half of the Roman Empire during the fifth century A.D., and who finally took and burnt Rome itself. So nearly all the old manuscript Bibles we have are later than the eighth century.

But not quite all. There is a copy of the complete Bible in Greek, written in the fourth century, in the library of the Pope's palace in Rome. The palace is called the Vatican, so the Bible is called the Codex Vaticanus. It has been in the Pope's library for centuries.

But there are two other copies, and we can be very proud of the fact that they are both in London, and can be seen in the British Museum by anyone who is interested. One is called the Codex Alexandrinus, and it was presented to King James I by the Patriarch of Constantinople, although it did not actually reach England until 1628, when Charles I was on the throne. A patriarch is a kind of archbishop of the Eastern, or Greek Church. The Patriarch of Constantinople had previously been Patriarch of Alexandria, and he is believed to have taken the manuscript from Alexandria to Constantinople with him. That is why it is called the Codex

Papyrus roll. A section of the papyrus of Ani

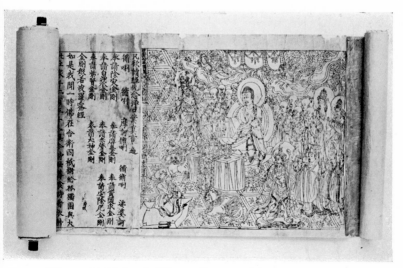

Wang-chieh's book. The earliest surviving printed book

SENATVSPOPVLVSQVEROMANVS
IMPCAESARIDIVINERVAEFNERVAE
TRAIANOAVGGERMDACICOPONTIF
MAXIMOTRIBPOTXVIIIMPVICOSVIPP
ADDECLARANDVMQVANTAEALTITVDINIS
MONSETLOCVSTANT̄ · · · IBVSSITEGESTVS

Inscription on Trajan's Column. From a cast in the Victoria and Albert Museum

Alexandrinus. It was probably written in Egypt in the early part of the fifth century A.D. After it arrived in England the book stayed in the royal library until the British Museum was founded, when George II gave it to the museum with other valuable books.

The arrival of the Codex Alexandrinus in England more than three hundred years ago caused great excitement among scholars, for it was the earliest copy of the Bible, or any part of it, that anyone in Britain had ever seen up to that time. In many ways the wording of it was different from the Bible with which English people at that time were familiar. I shall be telling you more about that later. From that time onwards scholars searched the old libraries and collections of books all over Europe in order to find any scraps that were left of ancient manuscripts of any part of the Bible, and they studied and compared and translated every bit they found.

Then, about a hundred years ago, the greatest and most exciting discovery of all was made. A young German scholar named Tischendorf began searching for ancient manuscripts in more out-of-the-way places than had been thought of before. In 1844 he arrived at a monastery on Mount Sinai. One day he saw a basket in which were a number of sheets of vellum on which there was some very early uncial writing. He was told that the sheets were going to be burnt. He asked if he might keep them and was told that he might. You can imagine his excitement when he examined them and found that they were forty-three leaves from an ancient copy of the Septuagint, and that they were at least a century older than the Alexandrinus, having been written in the fourth century.

Tischendorf took the sheets to Liepzig and put them in the university library. But he knew there were more and that the monks, when they saw how interested he was, had stopped destroying the book. He returned to the monastery from time to time, but could not get any news of the rest of the manuscript. Then, fifteen years after the original discovery, he was again in the monastery, working among the books, when on the very last evening of his stay he was talking to the steward about the Septuagint and the steward took a parcel wrapped in cloth from a shelf, unwrapped it—and there was the rest of the precious manuscript, a hundred and ninety-nine pages containing practically the whole of the Old and of the New Testaments.

Tischendorf was not allowed to take the manuscript away because the superintendent was absent at another monastery in Cairo, but Tischendorf hurried to him and the superintendent sent a rider on a camel to fetch the manuscript. Then the sheets were handed out one by one for Tischendorf to copy.

Tischendorf suggested that the monastery should present the precious manuscript to the Tsar of Russia, who was the protector of the Greek Church, and later he was allowed to take it to St. Petersburg (as Leningrad was called then), where he superintended the printing of it. The manuscript, which is called the Codex Sinaiticus because it was found on Mount Sinai, stayed in Russia until 1933. But its adventures were not over, for in 1933 the Soviet Government decided that they would sell it, and the British Government bought it for £100,000.

So now it can be seen in the British Museum, beside the Codex Alexandrinus and the fragments of the ancient papyrus codices found in Egypt and called the Chester-Beatty papyri—some of the oldest copies of the Bible, or any parts of it, that are to be seen anywhere in the world, except, of course, for the Old Testament scrolls found in Palestine in 1949, which are still being studied and discussed by scholars.

These two codices were written in Greek, as all the earliest complete Bibles were, but during the years following the acceptance of Christianity by Rome the Bible was translated into several languages. One was Coptic, which you remember was the language spoken by the natives of Egypt, the people descended from the Ancient Egyptians who had built the temples and pyramids, and who had made the original hiero-glyphic inscriptions. You remember that it was a knowledge of Coptic that helped Champollion to interpret the Rosetta Stone.

Several translations into Latin were made, but about A.D. 382 Pope Damasus asked a great scholar named Jerome (now called St. Jerome) to revise these translations, and produce a really reliable Latin version. St. Jerome made a fresh transla-tion into Latin from the Hebrew Old Testament, and used the oldest and best Greek manuscripts of the New Testament he could find for his translation of the New Testament. St. Jerome's Latin Bible was called the Vulgate and became the accepted Bible of Western Europe right through the Middle Ages, and is still the Bible of the Roman Catholic Church.

CHAPTER VII

★

Monks, and the Books they Made

From the very beginning of Christianity there were men who decided that they wanted to get away from the temptations and the luxury of cities and give all their time to worshipping God. So they went away into wild and lonely places and lived very simply, and sometimes very uncomfortably, in caves and places of that kind. We call such people hermits.

Some of the earliest hermits settled on the shores of the Red Sea and in the Egyptian desert. Often the hermits were joined by others who felt as they did, and groups of men settled down together. Such communities became what we now call monasteries.

Almost from the beginning monasteries seem to have had a certain number of books, chiefly, of course, parts of the Bible, service books, and books about Christianity.

There were a large number of monasteries in the eastern half of the Roman Empire. The whole of a peninsula at the northern end of the Aegean Sea called Mount Athos became covered with monasteries. Twenty of them are still in existence.

When the barbarian hordes swept over the western half of the Roman Empire and destroyed it, a few scholars, with their books, escaped to Constantinople and the monasteries of the East and there, for hundreds of years, some of the precious manuscripts of Ancient Greece and Rome were kept in safety, while most of the men and women of the West forgot their very existence.

But even though the Roman Empire collapsed in the fifth century A.D., Christianity, even in the West, was not destroyed. The Pope, whom the Christians of the West regarded as the head of the Church, lived on in Rome, and in time the pagan conquerors themselves became Christian.

But for centuries monasteries were the only places where men who did not want to live violent lives could read and study and think. It was in monasteries that some of the learning and culture of Ancient Rome and Greece was preserved, after the libraries and private collections of books in all the great cities of the Roman Empire had been destroyed.

In 528 St. Benedict founded a monastery at Monte Cassino in Italy, and within a few years there were Benedictine monasteries scattered all over Europe, including England, where they were established at Canterbury, York, Whitby, Glastonbury and other places.

Benedict laid down strict rules as to how his monks were to live. In particular they were not to be lazy and waste time, as idleness, he said, was an enemy of the soul. So when a monk had no other duties to perform he was to read, and the monks were to be read to at all meals and in the evenings.

Also, wrote Benedict, 'Every one is to have a book given out to him from the library at the beginning of Lent, which he is to read through, while two senior brethren are to go the rounds during reading hours to see that the monks are actually reading, and neither lounging nor gossiping. On Sundays all are to read throughout the day. . . .'

If the monks were to read they must have books. So in all monasteries monks spent a good deal of their time not only reading any books they had, or could borrow, but in making

Monks, and the Books they Made

copies for their own libraries, and to take with them when they went out to preach to and convert the heathen around them.

As more and more people were converted to Christianity the new churches that were built needed copies of the Bible, especially of the New Testament, and of books telling them how the services of the Church should be carried out. All these books were written in the monasteries.

So to learn what happened next in the story of the book it is the monasteries we must visit. And we shall find that during the thousand or so years, from about A.D. 500 to 1500, that we call the Middle Ages, monks working quietly in their cells or writing rooms produced many of the most beautiful books the world has ever known. Not only were these books perfectly and most beautifully written, but their pages were decorated with patterns and pictures in gold and all kinds of magnificent colours, painted by monks who were artists—often very great artists indeed.

We call books that are written by hand and decorated in this way 'illuminated manuscripts'. To illuminate, as you know, means to light up, and that is just what these wonderful pictures and decorations, with their glowing colours, seem to do to a page of writing. In the earliest illuminated manuscripts there are sometimes whole pages of pictures, with no writing on them at all, but in later books the decoration is part of the first, or initial, letter of a book or section, and the decoration is often very elaborate indeed. Not only is the letter itself made into an unusual decorative shape, but behind it, inside and all round it, is pattern and colour, which sometimes continues round the edge of the page, enclosing the writing in a framework of decoration.

In the Middle Ages every great monastery had a scriptorium or writing-room, where monks were always busy copying books, usually under the supervision of a chief scribe.

Each scribe had a stool, a steeply sloping desk, a cupboard, a cloth with which to protect his work from dust or too much sunlight, his pens, which were made from the quills of geese or similar birds, his pots of ink or colour, and his knife. With his knife he cut his pens to the shape and width he wanted,

A monk copying a book

and that is why we still call a small pocket-knife a penknife. He also used it to scrape the parchment if it got too smooth and wouldn't take the ink properly, or to make corrections when necessary.

The scribes were not allowed to have any lamps or candles in the scriptorium for fear of setting fire to valuable books, so they could only work during the hours of daylight. They were not allowed to speak to each other, so they learnt to communicate by a kind of sign language.

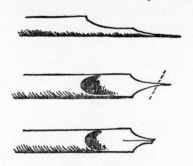

How a quill or reed pen is cut

The monks not only cut their own pens but they made their own inks and colours. Usually the inks in ancient illuminated manuscripts are as black, and the colours as bright, as they were when they were first put on the parchment, sometimes more than a thousand years ago. Here is a recipe from an old book explaining one way of making ink. You can see that it was not a quick or easy job.

'Dry for two to four hours the wood of thorn-tree picked in April or May. Peel the bark by beating the wood with mallets and soak it in water for eight days. Boil the water, adding bits of bark for a short time, and cook it down until it thickens. Then add wine and cook again. Place the liquid in pots in the sun until the black liquid purifies itself from the red dregs. Afterwards take small bags of parchment, or bladders, and, pouring into them the pure ink, hang them in the sun until all is dry. Then take from it what you want, dilute it with wine over the fire, and, adding to it a little vitriol, write.'

Colours were made in various ways. One shade of green ink was made from verdigris, while blue was often made from the blue stone called lapis lazuli, that you may sometimes have seen in jewellers' shop windows. Various chemicals, as well as barks and berries that sometimes had to come from

Four sheets of parchment stitched together

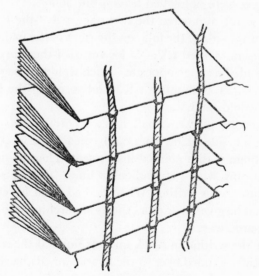

The quaternions tied to cords

overseas, were used for the other colours, but whatever the colour needed it had to be made in the monasteries by the monks themselves.

The gold that was often used in illuminated manuscripts was real gold. Sometimes it was beaten to a very thin sheet, cut to the shape that was needed, and fastened to the page over a sticky substance. Sometimes the gold was ground to a powder and mixed with white of egg to make a paint.

When a scribe was going to start work he was given four sheets of parchment, each nearly twice as wide as they were high—say ten inches by eighteen inches. Parchment is not quite so white and smooth on the side on which the hair originally grew as it is on the other side. The four sheets of parchment were put on top of one another with lighter and darker sides uppermost alternately, so that light sides faced light sides and dark sides faced dark sides. Then they were folded in the centre, thus making a book of eight leaves. But the leaves were not called leaves, but 'folios'.

The scribe numbered the first page 1.R.—the R meaning recto, or the side of the folio on the right of the fold. The next page was numbered 1.V.—V for verso, or the side on the left of the fold. The page opposite, which would be page 3 in our numbering, was number 2.R., and so on to the last page, which would be 8.V.

The scribe pricked small holes a certain distance apart down each side of his page and ruled horizontal lines between them with a pointed instrument. Then he marked off the margins with perpendicular lines. The lines were to guide him in his writing. When he had filled his eight folios he would be given four more sheets of parchment to deal with in the same way.

After the writing in black ink was finished the manuscript was usually handed over to the rubricator. Ruber means red in Latin, and the rubricator was a scribe who inserted initials

The ends of the cords threaded through wooden boards

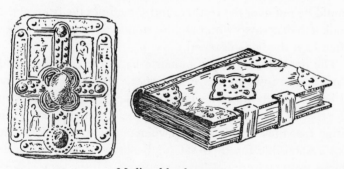

Medieval book-covers

or marginal instructions for priests in red. We still call the rules that are followed in carrying out Church services the rubric, because in ancient manuscripts they were written in red.

If the manuscript was to be illuminated it would be passed on to the artist whose business it was to paint and decorate it. The necessary spaces would, of course, have been left in the writing. Sometimes the same monk would be both scribe and illuminator, but it is very seldom that we know the names of the men who made these lovely books.

Each set of four sheets was stitched together down the centre fold, and was called a quaternion, from the Latin word for four, quatuor.

When all the quaternions were finished and placed one on top of another the ends of the threads that had stitched each one were tied round strong cords that were put across the backs of them all. The ends of the cords were then threaded through slots in two oak boards that formed the front and back covers of the book, and the ends of the cords were frayed out and flattened on to the board. The boards were then covered with leather, or sometimes with plates of silver or gold. Sometimes metal corners and other decorations would be put over the leather, and sometimes the front of the book was decorated with precious stones. Strong metal clasps often kept the book fastened.

The books belonging to monasteries in the early days did not stand in rows on shelves in a special room, as collections of books usually do now. They were kept in strong wooden chests with good locks, or lying on shelves in cupboards. In either case they were locked up when not in use, and someone was responsible for their safety. Books were very valuable things, so they were not left lying about. All the same, books were often lent by one monastery to another, so that they could be copied—though some people did not really care to let their valuable books out of their sight.

The bishop's book chest

A very learned abbot of a monastery at Ferrières in the ninth century was a great lover of books. Some of his letters have survived. In one he refuses to lend a book to a monk because the messenger who would have to carry it would have a dangerous journey on foot, and the book might be stolen or damaged. Another book, he says, is too large to go into a wallet, or be concealed in the messenger's clothes, and 'it might be a prey to robbers tempted by its beauty'. So he refuses to send that one either.

CHAPTER VIII

★

The Earliest Illuminated Manuscripts

The first country we must visit in our search for beautiful illuminated manuscripts is Ireland. Ireland was protected by its position on the western edge of Europe, and by the surrounding sea, from some of the turmoil that disturbed the rest of Europe.

In the fourth century a sixteen-year-old Christian boy was captured in Gaul (which is now France) and was carried away to heathen Ireland as a slave. After six years he managed to escape and later he became a monk and later still a bishop. But he kept thinking of the men and women he had known in Ireland, and at last he returned to the country in which he had been a slave and began the work of converting the Irish to Christianity. He founded many churches and monasteries, and baptized many thousands of people before he died in A.D. 463. His name was Succat, but the Pope gave him the name of Patricius, and he is known to us as St. Patrick.

In time Ireland became a great centre of learning. Her monasteries and schools were famous and she was called 'the island of saints and scholars'. Students travelled to Ireland from other parts of Europe in order to learn from her wise men, and Irish missionaries went out from Ireland to other countries teaching and preaching. And in the Irish monasteries books were written and illuminated that are some of the finest that have ever been made.

The Irish valued their lovely books and sometimes they made a special box, or shrine, for an especially fine one. These book-shrines were called 'cundachs', and sometimes they were very valuable indeed. The oldest one that has survived held a copy of the Gospels. It was made of plates of bronze ornamented with patterns cut out in silver and gold and riveted on to the bronze. The design shows an angel, a lion, an ox, and an eagle, which are the symbols of St. Matthew, St. Mark, St. Luke and St. John, the Evangelists who wrote the four Gospels.

One of the most famous of the Irish books is called the *Book of Kells*. It was written at the monastery of Kells in County Antrim, and is now in the library of Trinity College, Dublin. We do not know exactly when it was written, but it was probably about A.D. 700.

The people who lived in Ireland were called Celts. Celtic art is not noted for the naturalness of its figures and portraits of human beings. You would probably feel that the saints and angels that appear in the *Book of Kells* are stiff and awkward looking. But what Celtic art is famous for is the intricacy of its geometrical designs—designs made up from squares and circles, and especially from interlacing ribbons and spirals which twist and turn in and out and around each other in a most bewildering way.

Here and there among the coiling ribbons in the *Book of Kells* a little head suddenly appears, or the lengthened, grotesque body of an animal or bird becomes part of the design. But if the bird is a dove, or the animal a lamb, it will not be made grotesque, because the monks believed that these were sacred, and that the devil could take the shape of any other bird or beast, but not that of a lamb or dove. Near the lower corner of one of the most beautiful of the initials in the *Book of Kells* is a space which, instead of being filled with interlacing lines, contains an unexpected little picture of two rats nibbling at a round cake, while two cats, each with a rat on its back, look on. One can gaze at a page of the *Book of Kells* for hours without coming to an end of its surprises.

Irish monks carried the art of writing and illuminating to Scotland and Northern England. An old story tells us that it happened in this way.

St. Columba (or Columcille), who founded several monasteries in Ireland (including the one at Kells), was himself a scribe. One day while he was visiting St. Finnian in a monastery in the north of Ireland he borrowed a copy of St. Finnian's Book of Psalms. St. Columba wanted a copy of the book, so he used to sit up at night copying it, and a mysterious light, the legend tells us, filled the room so that he could see to do the work. One night an inquisitive monk peeped through the keyhole of Columba's room to see what he was doing, and a stork which was always with Columba thrust his long bill through the keyhole and blinded him.

When Columba had finished copying the book St. Finnian, who knew by now what he had been doing, refused to let him take the copy away. But Columba would not give it up. As the two couldn't agree they took the dispute to the High King of Ireland at Tara. He declared against Columba, and said, 'To every cow its calf; to every book its copy.' But Columba refused to accept this judgment, or to give up the copy he had made, and the quarrel between himself and Finnian became fiercer than ever until at last it ended in a great battle, in A.D. 561, at a place called Culdremhue, in which there was much bloodshed. Columba was blamed for all this trouble, and he was banished from Ireland.

How much truth there is in this story we do not know, but one thing is certain, Columba did leave Ireland with twelve followers, and they landed on the rocky island that we now

A page from the Lindisfarne Gospels

call Iona, off the west coast of Scotland. Here Columba founded a monastery in A.D. 563, and from Iona the Irish missionary-monks set out to convert the fierce Picts of the mainland, and later the people of Northern England. He founded other monasteries, under the control of the chief one at Iona, before he died in A.D. 597.

About thirty-five years after the death of Columba a monk named Aidan, who had been brought up at Iona, was sent to Northumbria at the request of the King, whose name was Oswald, to become Bishop of Northumbria. King Oswald and Aidan built a monastery and church on the lonely island of Lindisfarne about three miles from the coast of Northumberland, and there Aidan lived when he was not travelling about the mainland teaching and preaching. Aidan and his companions brought with them to Northumbria the skill and learning they had acquired at Iona, and soon books were being produced there, just as they were in other monasteries. And at Lindisfarne was written, about fifty years after Aidan's death in A.D. 651, a book that is one of the most beautiful that has survived from these early times.

It is called the Lindisfarne Gospels, and is one of the treasures of the British Museum. Like the *Book of Kells*, it consists of the four Gospels in Latin, and at the beginning of each Gospel is a full-page portrait showing what the artist thought the evangelist who wrote that particular Gospel looked like.

There are also many pages on which are beautiful illuminated initials, with intricate interlacing patterns, similar to those found in the *Book of Kells*. The figures in the Lindisfarne Gospels are rather more natural than those in the *Book of Kells*. That may be because the people at Lindisfarne had seen books which had come into England from Rome, brought by missionaries who came after St. Augustine had landed in Kent and begun the conversion of the south of England. The figures in these books from the south of

Europe were more life-like than those in the Celtic books.

Many years after the Lindisfarne Gospels was written some-one wrote a note in it in Anglo-Saxon. The translation is:

'Thou living God, be thou mindful of Eadfrith, Aethelwald, Billfrith, and Aldred, a sinner. These four have, with God's help, been engaged upon this book.'

It may have been Aldred who wrote these words, at the same time that he made certain other notes in the book in Anglo-Saxon. Eadfrith was Bishop of Lindisfarne from 698 to 721, and it is believed that he was the scribe who wrote the book and the artist who painted the pictures. Aethelwald, who was bishop from 724 to 740, may have been responsible for the binding, and Billfrith may have cut the jewels that were embedded in metal on the cover—all of which have disappeared long ago.

The book has had some exciting adventures. In the year 875 the monks of Lindisfarne had to fly from their island be-cause of the Danes who were pillaging and destroying every-where. They took with them their two most precious treasures, the coffin containing the body of St. Cuthbert, who had died in 687 and been buried at Lindisfarne, and their copy of the Gospels. They wandered for a long time trying to find a safe resting place. At one time they tried to get across to Ireland, but immediately they left the shore a great storm sprang up, and, according to the legend, the precious book fell over-board. Taking this as a sign that God did not want the body of St. Cuthbert to leave England, they put back to the shore. The ancient chronicle tells us that in the night St. Cuthbert appeared to one of the monks and told him to search in the sea for the book. Next day they began the search and found that the tide had gone out much farther than usual. About three miles from the shore they found the book quite un-damaged. After this the book was usually called the 'Book of St. Cuthbert'.

The monks at last found a resting place on a hill called Dunholm. They built a church over the spot where they buried St. Cuthbert, a church that afterwards became Durham Cathedral.

You can see the Lindisfarne Gospels in the British Museum, and in other parts of England there are a few other books dating from those early days before the Danes began to ravage England. In the library of Lichfield Cathedral there is one called the Gospels of St. Chad, and there is a very ancient copy of the Gospels in the Bodleian Library, Oxford, and another in the library of Lambeth Palace, the Archbishop of Canterbury's London home.

Of course, the books that were written in Anglo-Saxon times were not all copies of the Bible, or parts of it, or of church service books, although a great many were. Here and there learned men wrote books of their own. One of the most famous of these men was Bede, who is generally called the Venerable Bede. He was born at Monkwearmouth in Durham about A.D. 673, and studied at a monastery there under another famous scholar called Benedict Biscop before going to another monastery at Jarrow. Bede was a very industrious and studious man, and we are told that as well as learning Latin and Greek and reading Latin and Greek literature, he studied Hebrew, medicine and astronomy. But he wrote books himself as well, in Latin—books about the saints and about the Bible, hymns and books on grammar and history. His most famous book is his *Ecclesiastical History* of England, which tells us almost all we know about England in those faraway times, up to A.D. 731.

I expect you all know the story of how Bede translated St. John's Gospel from Latin into Anglo-Saxon, dictating the words to a young scribe who sat by his bed, and how he died after dictating the last words.

The earliest of the Anglo-Saxon poets was Caedmon,

whom Bede tells us about. He worked in the monastery at Whitby, of which St. Hilda was Abbess. One night he had a vision, and was told that he must sing about the Creation of the world. Caedmon said he could not sing and that he had no learning. But he was again told to sing, and he found that the words came. Afterwards he wrote the words of his songs, and he and those who followed him and who wrote in the same way, produced the first English poetry.

One man who did a great deal for learning and literature in Anglo-Saxon times was King Alfred himself. He studied Latin, and translated into his own language books that he thought would be valuable to the people of England—books such as Bede's *Ecclesiastical History*.

By the eighth century the monasteries of England, especially those of the north-east, had become famous centres of learning. In some of them there were fine libraries, though the books in them were usually those that had been written by Christian scholars and teachers. The great literature of Ancient Greece and Rome was often neglected or forgotten, because it had been written by people who were not Christians.

Sometimes when monks wanted parchment on which to make yet another copy of some religious writing they washed and scraped away the ancient Greek or Latin writing from some rare pagan book and wrote on that. But fortunately for us it was almost impossible to get rid of the old writing entirely, and modern treatment has brought some of it to light again. We call manuscripts that have been cleaned and re-used in this way 'palimpsests'.

There were, of course, a few scholar-monks who felt differently about the ancient non-Christian literature. A library was founded in York in the eighth century that was considered the finest in Europe. It was founded by a man named Alcuin, and he himself said that it contained 'all Latin literature, all that Greece had handed on to the Romans, all that the Hebrew people had received from on high, all that Africa with clear-flowing light had given'. But Alcuin was a very exceptional person.

In Europe about this time a great king of the Franks called Charles, whom we call Charlemagne, or Charles the Great, managed to make himself master of much of Central Europe which had been part of the Roman Empire three hundred or more years before. On Christmas Day in the year 800 the Pope in Rome crowned him Emperor, and they called his new dominion the 'Holy Roman Empire'.

But Charlemagne was not only a great conqueror. He was keenly interested in learning, and he wanted to help the people of Europe to live more civilized lives. Many years before he was crowned Emperor he persuaded Alcuin to leave York and join his court and help him to found schools and centres of learning. Later Alcuin became Abbot of the Abbey of St. Martin at Tours, and the school he founded there became famous all over Europe.

Charlemagne saw that there could be no learning without books, so he gave orders that all Church literature, and all that was left of Greek and Roman literature, should be revised and re-copied.

This led to tremendous activity among the scribes. It led, too, to the development of a different way of writing. You remember that in the days of Ancient Rome all writing was done in capital letters. There were the square capitals, the rustic capitals and later the more rounded uncials. In Ireland a kind of uncial writing had developed which we call half-uncial, and this way of writing had been introduced into England by the monks from Ireland. But it was still all in capital letters, or majuscules as they are called. Now, however, in the days of Charlemagne, a way of writing with small letters, or minuscules, which were quite distinct from

the capital letters, developed. For the first time, too, writing
was divided into sentences and paragraphs, and a capital
letter was put at the beginning of the sentence and a full stop
at the end.

These first small letters are called 'Carolingian minuscules'
because they first came into general use in the days of Charlemagne.

$$Carolingian$$

Carolingian minuscules

Other changes gradually took place, too. You remember
that the Roman alphabet had no letter U or W. But in
writing V quickly the scribes often tended to make it look
like a U. For a long time either form of the letter was used
where we should use a V or a U, but gradually the two letters
came to represent different sounds, and U took its place in
the alphabet just before V. About the same time scribes took
to writing two V's joined together to represent the sound we
call W, and that letter, too, took its place in the alphabet.

Another change was that people began to write figures in a
different way. We call the figures we use now 'Arabic' numerals, and the reason is that they originated in India and the
Arabs learnt them there and introduced them into Spain.
The Arabs, or Moors, were ruling Spain at that time. But
Europeans did not begin to use the Arabic figures for some
hundreds of years. A man named Leonardo Fibonacci, who
lived in Pisa, was the first to write in praise of the new
system early in the thirteenth century.

The Arabs indicated the first three figures by making one,
two, or three little horizontal strokes. Our figures two and
three have developed through the scribes writing the strokes
quickly without lifting the pen, and so joining them together.

For some reason the little stroke for one got turned round and became vertical.

Writing with minuscules (small letters) as well as majuscules (capital letters) and the new way of separating sentences and paragraphs, and of punctuating, soon spread all over Europe. But each country developed its own individual style, so that experts can often tell just where and when a manuscript was written.

In particular, a style developed in northern Europe which nowadays we call Gothic, or Black Letter. The letters were made very narrow and straight, and were packed up close together. The upright strokes were made very thick and the others very thin, so that the effect of the writing on the page was very black. Although to us this kind of writing does not seem very clear or easy to read, it became very popular, and after two or three centuries it took the place of all other styles.

abcdefghijklmnopqrstuvwxyz

The Gothic alphabet

About the time that Alcuin and his scribes were developing new ways of writing at Tours and other places, in Britain the Danes had begun to invade and to rob and murder and destroy wherever they landed.

Lindisfarne was not the only monastery to be abandoned or destroyed.

At last, in 878, Alfred, the King of Wessex, after defeating a Danish army under Guthrum, made an agreement with the Danes that they would stay in the north and north-east of England and leave the south and south-west alone, and that they would become Christians.

Alfred's chief city was Winchester, and when England became one nation under one king, Winchester became the capital of the whole country. Towards the end of the tenth century two monasteries were founded in the city, the Old Minster and the New Minster. From these monasteries, during the time between their foundation and the Norman Conquest, there flowed a stream of lovely illuminated manuscripts that brought great fame to Winchester. Some of them have survived.

One of the finest belongs to the Duke of Devonshire and is at Chatsworth House in Derbyshire. It is called the Benedictional of St. Aethelwold, and contains the forms of blessing to be used by the bishop at different seasons of the year. It has thirty full-page pictures, as well as many other richly decorated pages, including two in which the letters are written in pure gold. These golden pages are especially interesting because they tell us that Aethelwold, who was Bishop of Winchester from 963 until 984, had given orders to 'a certain monk' to write the book, and the writing ends with a request that all who look at the book will pray for 'Godeman, the writer'. So we are told not only the date, more or less, when the book was written, but the name of the scribe who wrote it. We do not know, unfortunately, who painted the pictures.

Another famous manuscript from Winchester, which you can see in the British Museum, is the Charter of King Edgar to New Minster, dated 968. It is a book in which there is a picture of King Edgar himself, with the Virgin and St. Peter. Above in the sky is Christ with four angels. The king is holding up his arms, and in his right hand is the book, the Charter of the newly dedicated Minster, which he is offering to God. This is the earliest picture from Winchester that we have.

Beautiful manuscripts were being written and illuminated during this time at other places, of course, besides Winchester. There were two monasteries, for instance, at Canterbury, and others at Durham, Bury St. Edmunds, Hereford, and elsewhere.

＊

Books in England after the Normans Came

After the Normans had conquered England in 1066 they built, or rebuilt, a great many churches and monasteries. Soon beautiful illuminated books were being made in monasteries all over the country. Sometimes scribes and illuminators, instead of working in the scriptorium, worked by themselves in little cells, or carrels as they were called, built against the windows of the cloisters. They were quite narrow—'no greater than from one stanchell of the wyndowe to another', an old sixteenth-century account tells us —which means that there was one against each section, or 'light', of the big windows. Each little cell was about as big as a sentry-box and contained a desk and stool for one monk. Against the other walls of the cloister were the cupboards in which books were kept—it was, in fact, the abbey library.

Monks do not seem to have minded working in solitude. One, whose name was Nicholas, certainly did not, for he wrote, 'It must not be supposed that my little tenement is to be despised, for it is a place to be desired, and is pleasant to look upon and comfortable for retirement. It is filled with most choice and divine books, at the delightful view of which I feel contempt for the vanity of the world.'

Now that the whole country was Christian and there were churches and priests everywhere, it was not necessary for monks to go from place to place teaching people about Christianity. They did not need so many copies of the Gospels, so more time was given to writing huge copies of the whole Bible, sometimes in three or four large volumes, for use in the monastic and parish churches.

Some of these early Bibles have survived and are in the libraries of such places as Durham and Winchester Cathedrals. Many of them have wonderful pictures painted in the initial letters of each book. One marvellous copy of the Bible at Durham, in four volumes, which was written in the twelfth century, is not complete because someone, about two hundred years ago, actually cut out some of the pictures and gave them to some children to play with!

One of the most famous Bible illuminations is in a Bible in the library of Trinity College, Cambridge. The first words of the Book of Genesis, in Latin, are 'In principio' (In the beginning). The letter I in the Bible at Cambridge has been made very large indeed, and in it there are thirty-eight tiny pictures of the chief events in the Bible, both from the Old and the New Testaments.

Besides Bibles and service books (or Missals, as they are called) you would have found in nearly every monastery from the thirteenth century onwards a book called the *Legenda Aurea* (the Golden Legend). It was a book about the saints, telling the story of their lives and the miracles they were believed to have performed. The *Legenda Aurea* was written by a Dominican monk named Jacobus de Voragine who lived from about 1230 to about 1298, and became Archbishop of Genoa. He wrote the book in Latin, of course, but soon after his death it was translated into French.

By this time, the twelfth and thirteenth centuries, books were not used only in monasteries and churches. Wealthy people liked to possess beautiful illuminated books, or to give them as presents to other people—but they had to order the book they wanted, and then wait a very long time while the scribe wrote it out, and the illuminator painted the pictures and the binders bound it, and such books were very expensive.

During the thirteenth and early part of the fourteenth centuries the most popular illuminated book was the Apocalypse. That is the name which is sometimes given to the Book of Revelation, which is the last book in the Bible, and which is said to have been written by St. John. If you read the Book of Revelation some time you will find that it is a description of a kind of vision and that it is full of hidden meanings, and of symbols. It gave the artists a fine chance to use their imaginations, and they produced some wonderful books full of lovely pictures. About forty copies of the Apocalypse from this period have survived. The very best one is in the library of Trinity College, Cambridge. It is a very big book, each folio measuring seventeen inches by twelve inches, and it is believed that it was made for Eleanor of Provence, who married our King Henry III in 1236. Four artists worked on the many paintings, but we do not know any of their names.

An inscription in the book tells us that in 1649, four hundred years after it was written, it was in the possession of a lady named Anne Sadleir. I expect you remember that in 1649 Charles I was beheaded and England became a Commonwealth under Cromwell, so things were in a state of great confusion. Many beautiful things, such as stained-glass windows, pictures, statues and church books were being destroyed by the Puritans. So Anne gave the book to Ralph Brownrigg, Bishop of Exeter, and asked him to look after it and, she wrote, 'when times are better settled (which God hasten) it is with my other bookes and my coines given to Trinitie Colledge in Cambridge, God in his good time restore her with her sister Oxford to their pristine happiness, the Vulgar People to their former obedience, our God bles and restore

Charles II and make him like his most glorious Father.
Amen.'

There is no doubt at all that Anne Sadleir was a Royalist!

Another kind of book that was very popular about this
time was called a Bestiary, and it was a very odd sort of book
indeed. It was a kind of natural history and book of morals
combined. But the natural history was not like anything
we learn to-day. In the Middle Ages very few people had
been far from their homes, so they were ready to believe that
absolutely anything was possible in far-away lands. They had
no difficulty in accepting dragons that breathed out flame
and smoke, centaurs that were half men and half horses,
salamanders that could live in fire, ant-lions that had the fore-
part of a lion and the hind-part of an ant—and other surprising creatures.

In the Bestiaries the strange ways (sometimes true but
often quite imaginary) of real animals, and of these other
fantastic creatures, were described, and a moral lesson of
some kind was drawn from them. For instance, the reader is
told that an elephant which has a load on its back cannot rise
without help, and that in the same way man, who carries a
load of sin, cannot rise without Christ. And he is told that the
salamander can live in fire, just as the Christian can resist the
fire of temptation.

The artists who illuminated the Bestiaries had plenty of
opportunity to use their imaginations, and they created some
really extraordinary and fearsome creatures, with the strang-
est habits. The Bestiaries themselves ceased to be popular
after the beginning of the fourteenth century, but weird, dis-
torted animals continued to appear, not only in illuminated
manuscripts but in carving and sculpture, for generations.
Outside many of our ancient cathedrals and churches you
will see water spouts in the form of hideous animal or half-
human heads protruding from just below the edge of the

roof (they are called gargoyles), and inside you may find curious animals such as never really existed carved under the tip-up seats (the misericordes, as they are called) in the choir.

This does not mean that the artists of the time could not paint or carve real animals and birds very naturally and beautifully when they wanted to. They could and they very often did.

By the end of the thirteenth century another kind of book had become very popular. It was the Psalter, or book of psalms. Psalters had been written from the earliest days of Christianity—you remember that the book St. Columba is said to have copied was a book of psalms—for in the church services of the Middle Ages the whole of the psalms were said, or sung, every week. But the Psalters of the thirteenth and early fourteenth centuries contained far more than just the psalms, and they were the most generously and elaborately decorated of all the books made during the Middle Ages. The first part of the book was a calendar of the Church's year, showing the saints' days and the festivals of the Church. The names of the chief saints and festivals were written in red and were sometimes decorated with gold; the others were written in ordinary black ink. That is why we still speak of an important or exciting day as a red-letter day. On the margins round the calendar are scenes showing the work that people did during the different seasons of the year.

Next, very often, came several pages of pictures, sometimes of scenes from the life of Christ. Then came the beginning of the psalms, and the page on which most care and labour was lavished. It is called the Beatus page, because the first words are 'Beatus sit' (Blessed be the man). The psalms are divided into sections for each day's worship, and there is usually a richly ornamented page at the beginning of each section. Next come the canticles, or sacred songs of the Church, which also formed part of the daily services, and sometimes a number of litanies and prayers.

It is very seldom that we know the name of the scribe responsible for a Psalter, but the monk who both wrote the words and painted the pictures in one very early one has not only told us his name but has painted us a picture of himself at work. He was Eadwine, and was chief of the scribes in a monastery in Canterbury about the middle of the twelfth century—that is, about one hundred years after the Norman Conquest. In his picture Eadwine shows himself sitting in a chair which is carved with round-headed openings something like the windows in Norman churches. He is dressed in the white habit of his Order, and has the shaved head of a monk. The open book rests on a desk similar to the chair, but partly covered with a cloth, which Eadwine doubtless puts over the book when he is not working at it. In his right hand he holds his pen, and in his left his small knife.

It would be interesting to know how long Eadwine took to write the six hundred pages, each measuring eighteen inches by thirteen inches, and to paint the pictures, but he does not tell us. At the end of the book are two interesting little maps which show us just what a monastery was like round about the year 1150. On one is shown the church; the chapter house (the room in which the business of the monastery was discussed); the kitchen; the refectory (where the monks ate their meals); the guest-room; the infirmary (for monks who were ill) and its chapel; the bath; the brewery; the herb garden; the well; the granary (where the grain was kept); and the vinery. The other plan shows how water was carried by underground pipes to different parts of the monastery.

One of the finest Psalters ever made is called Queen Mary's Psalter, and is in the British Museum. It was not made for a Queen Mary, but probably for King Edward I or Edward II. We do not know quite where it was made, or anything about its early history. But in the middle of the sixteenth century, when there was a lot of disagreement between Protestants and Catholics, a Customs official named Baldwin Smith stopped someone from smuggling it out of the country, and presented it to Queen Mary Tudor, who was on the throne of England at that time. It stayed in the royal library for two hundred years; then King George II gave it, with other books, to the new British Museum.

This wonderful book contains more than a thousand pictures of many different kinds. They are believed to be the work of one man, though no one, of course, knows who he was. He was a very great artist indeed, and this amazing book must have kept him busy for many years of his life. Some people believe that he was not a monk, and this is quite possible as by the beginning of the fourteenth century, when this book was written, beautiful manuscripts were being made outside the monasteries as well as inside them.

Psalters were written and illuminated in all monasteries, but towards the end of the thirteenth century the monasteries of East Anglia suddenly took the lead, and for some years they produced the best and finest Psalters that have ever been made anywhere. There are about thirty Psalters of this period in existence, and quite two-thirds of them were made in East Anglia. You can see some of them in the British Museum. One, for instance, is called the St. Omer Psalter. It was ordered about the year 1325 by a member of a family named St. Omer, who lived in Norfolk, but it was not finished until nearly a hundred years later, when it may possibly have been completed for Humphrey, Duke of Gloucester, who was the youngest son of King Henry IV. Its Beatus page is one of the very best in any Psalter.

A very famous Psalter that was once described as 'the most sumptuous English fourteenth-century manuscript in existence' was ordered by Thomas, Vicar of Gorleston, in Norfolk, and may have been made at the Priory of St. Andrew at Gorleston. Thomas gave it to John of Aylestoun, Abbot of the Benedictine Abbey of Hulme, Norfolk. Later it found its way to Douai, in France, where it was preserved for many years, so that it is always known as the Douai Psalter. But, alas, it is no longer one of the most perfect of the East Anglian Psalters. In the war of 1914–18, when the Germans were advancing on Douai, the people who had charge of the manuscript buried it in the ground for safety. But when it was dug up after the war they found that it had been ruined by damp.

Disasters like this must have happened to many of the precious books of the past, only we don't know about them.

Beautiful illuminated manuscripts were often made for kings or queens. In some cases, even if we don't know for whom they were made, we know into whose hands they came at some later time. There is a Psalter now at Exeter College, Oxford, which was made for Humphrey de Bohun (pronounced Boon) whose daughter Mary married Henry of Bolingbroke. Five years after her death Henry became King Henry IV, and the Psalter, which Mary had probably inherited from her father, remained in the royal family. On a fly-leaf in the book is written 'Thys boke ys myn, Elisabeth ye quene'. This Elisabeth was the wife of Henry VII and the mother of Henry VIII. Below is written 'Thys boke ys myn, Katherine the quene', showing that the Psalter later passed to Queen Katherine of Aragon, the first wife of Henry VIII.

Although Psalters were religious books and contained a great many pictures of scenes from the Bible and of saints and prophets, they often contained pictures of people doing ordinary everyday things as well. The calendar part of the book usually had pictures of people doing the work that was suited to the particular month, such as ploughing, reaping, beating oak trees to make acorns fall for pig-food, pruning and planting trees, and scores of other activities. Then there are hunting scenes and pictures of people taking part in sports that we should not care much for now, such as bear-baiting and playing games like draughts and ninepins. There are people playing musical instruments and dancing, and others on horseback tilting at each other with lances.

In the margins there are often grotesque drawings of all kinds of extraordinary animals, though there are also some very beautiful drawings of real animals and birds in some of the books.

Some of the pictures are very funny. One Psalter has a picture of a fox dressed up as a bishop and preaching to a number of ducks, and another of the funeral of a rabbit, with two dogs acting as bearers. Another has illustrations of a very old problem of a man who had to take some food, a lamb, and a wolf across a river, and could only take one at a time. But he could not leave the wolf and the lamb together, or the lamb and the food. Do you know how he solved the problem?

In the same Psalter is a picture of a woman chasing a fox which is running away with a hen.

A Psalter that is more famous than any other for its pictures of everyday life in the fourteenth century is the Luttrell Psalter, which is also in the British Museum. Almost every subject you can imagine is dealt with somewhere in this amazing book. There is an acrobat carrying a woman on his shoulders, a doctor with his patient, performing animals, a cat with a mouse, a fox stalking a goose, and many other similar things. Then there is a whole series of farming scenes, from which we learn a great deal about the implements that were used in the fourteenth century, and another series showing the preparation of a dinner from the roasting of meat and vegetables in the kitchen to the carving and serving of the meal. The diners are believed to be Sir Geoffrey Luttrell, for whom the Psalter was made, his wife Agnes, Sir Geoffrey's chaplain and his confessor, and three guests.

The Luttrell Psalter was written about 1340. The next manuscripts that have survived were not written until about thirty years later. Possibly this may have been one of the results of the plague called the Black Death which caused the deaths of so many people, including, of course, monks. The art of producing beautiful books never revived in East Anglia.

The next really important illuminated manuscript is an enormous Bible, one of the largest manuscripts known. It is called King Richard II's Bible. The pages measure just over twenty-four and a half inches by seventeen inches. It is a copy of the Vulgate. You remember that the Vulgate is the name given to the Latin translation that St. Jerome made from the Greek Bible in the fourth century in Rome. King Richard II's Bible is beautifully written and illuminated, and it contains a number of pictures that are supposed to represent St. Jerome writing the original Vulgate.

Westminster Abbey has a fine book that may have been connected with Richard II, too. It is a Coronation Book and may have been written for the Coronation of Richard and his wife. There is a picture in the book of a king and queen being crowned which some people think represents Richard and his wife, Anne of Bohemia.

During the fifteenth century Psalters were not quite so popular as they had been earlier, but many people liked to have another kind of book for private worship. It was called a Book of Hours. The most beautifully illuminated Books of Hours were written and painted in France and Flanders. One is called the Bedford Book of Hours because it belonged to John, Duke of Bedford, who was King Henry V's brother. It is in the British Museum. Another very lovely one, which was made in England, though we do not know where, is called 'The Hours of Elisabeth the Quene' because, like the

Psalter you read about just now, it was possessed at one time by Henry VII's wife, Elizabeth of York, and the words 'Elisabeth ye quene' are written in it.

Some beautiful service books (or Missals as they are called) have come down to us from the Middle Ages. One is called the Sherborne Missal because it was made for Sherborne Abbey. The artist who painted the pictures in it was a monk named John Siferwas and he was extraordinarily clever at painting birds of all kinds. Sometimes he painted a picture of himself in the Missal, and wrote under it 'Soli Deo honor et gloria' (To God alone be honour and glory).

He also painted an almost full-page picture of the Virgin and Child under a canopy, with, kneeling below them, the Bishop of Salisbury; the Abbot of Sherborne; the illuminator, John Siferwas, himself; and the scribe. As it happens we know the scribe's name, too. In fact he seems to have been determined that we should know it, and should understand what hard work he had done, for he tells us several times that 'John Whas, monk, laboured at writing this book'. In one place he writes, 'The name of the writer is John Whas, good and fair,' and in another, 'John Whas, monk, laboured at writing this book, and through rising early greatly exhausted his strength'.

Poor John Whas! Perhaps he got very tired of his long task before it was finished. The men who had the skill to paint the wonderful pictures which we see in illuminated manuscripts must have loved their work and found it thrilling and interesting all the time; but the endless copying of page after page which the scribes had to do must often have been very tedious.

Scribes who were not monks and who worked for private employers, copying whatever books they wanted, were not very well paid. Some scribes travelled about from place to place wherever they were needed or could find work. Others were employed by some particular nobleman, and perhaps had a lodging in his house.

Other scribes besides John Whas occasionally wrote what they really felt about their work, usually at the end when they had finished and their feelings were a mixture of relief and weariness. One wrote simply (in Latin, of course), 'I have made an end at last and my weary hand can rest', and another, 'Praise to Thee, O Christ, now when the "End" brings quiet to hand and pen'.

But others expressed themselves more strongly. 'The Book being finished, let us break the bones of our master', wrote one, and 'Now that I an end have made see that what I'm owed is paid', wrote another, while yet another writes as though he is very glad indeed to see the end of his task— 'Here's good-bye to pens and ink, now, for God's sake, let me drink'.

Sometimes scribes would make little comments at the side of the manuscript, or add a little bit of their own. On the margin of a copy of the Gospels, an Irish monk of the eighth century wrote a poem about his cat, Pangur Ban. This is the first verse, as translated from the Latin by Mr. Robin Flower:

> '*I and Pangur Ban, my cat,*
> '*Tis a like task we are at;*
> *Hunting mice is his delight,*
> *Hunting words I sit all night.*'

So in various ways the scribes tried to relieve the tediousness of their work, and no doubt many of them grumbled.

CHAPTER X

★

Englishmen Begin to Write in English

The illuminated manuscripts you have been reading about were books connected with the Church or with religion, such as Gospels, Psalters, Missals, Books of Hours and so on, and they were all written in Latin.

For two or three hundred years after the Norman Conquest the English language had quite a struggle to survive. All documents connected with law and government and religion were written in Norman-French, or in Latin, and every well-educated person learnt Latin as a matter of course.

Even new books that did not deal with religion, law or government were also written in Latin at first. One very famous book that appeared in the middle of the twelfth century was a kind of imaginary history of the Britons. It was written by a Welshman named Geoffrey of Monmouth, who later became Bishop of St. Asaph. Geoffrey said that his history was a translation into Latin of a very old book written in the language of the ancient Britons, or Celts, but no such book has ever been found.

It is believed that Geoffrey's book is partly a record of old legends and tales that had been handed down from one generation to another, and is partly written from his own imagination. It tells us about a hero called Brutus, whom Geoffrey claims was the ancestor of the Britons, and it tells a great deal about an even greater hero, King Arthur of the Britons, who, according to the book, lived in the seventh century. Geoffrey tells us that King Arthur conquered the Anglo-Saxons, the Picts and Scots, the people of Ireland, Scandinavia, Iceland, Gaul, and even of Rome itself.

No one knows for certain whether King Arthur ever really lived at all, but Geoffrey's stories about him spread all over England and France, and other writers wrote songs and stories about him in Latin and French.

But although nearly all books were written in Latin, the Saxons continued to use their own language among themselves, and towards the end of the twelfth century books in English began to appear. They were usually translations from French and Latin books, and were mostly sermons or prayers or books about the Bible, which people who did not know Latin could not read for themselves. At the end of the twelfth century a priest named Layamon translated a book based on Geoffrey of Monmouth's *History* into the English of his time, and during the next century or so other stories of adventure, legends and poems were translated into English.

Gradually Norman-French was used less and less and in time all the people of England spoke English. After 1350 French was no longer used by teachers in schools, as it had been before, and after 1362 English was used in the law courts. In 1399 the king, Henry IV, addressed Parliament in English for the first time.

Although some learned men continued for many years to write in Latin, from the fourteenth century onwards there were always Englishmen writing in their own language—English.

The name of one of the first and also one of the very greatest of the English poets was Geoffrey Chaucer. Chaucer was born in London about the year 1340. He lived a very active life, and mixed with all kinds of people. First he was a page at the king's court. Then he became a soldier and fought in France and was a prisoner for a time. After he got back to England he entered the service of John o' Gaunt, and was sent abroad several times, to France and Flanders and Italy. Later he was made Customs Officer in the Port of London, and later Clerk of the Royal Works, which meant that he was in charge of the repairs to royal palaces and chapels, the Tower of London and similar buildings. He became a Member of the House of Commons, too. Yet, in spite of all the many things he had to do, Chaucer found time to write some of the finest poetry ever written in English. I am sure you know the most famous of his works, the *Canterbury Tales*, in which he describes a number of people who are travelling to Canterbury on a pilgrimage, and who pass the time by telling each other stories.

Another well-known writer of the fourteenth century was a very different kind of man from Chaucer. His name was William Langland, and he was born in a village in Shropshire. His early life was lived among poor peasants, and even though, later, he lived in London, he went on thinking about them and being sorry for them. He knew that they were terribly poor and hard-worked and ignorant, and he felt that the Church and the monasteries cared more about their own riches and their own church services than they did about helping and teaching the people. He tried to express all that he felt in a great poem, which he worked on from time to time for thirty years. It is called *The Vision of Piers Plowman*. In it Langland described a number of dreams, or visions, he had in which he saw a 'field full of folk' of all kinds—rich and poor, ignorant and learned, good and bad. They were trying to find Truth, and their guide was Piers, or Peter, the ploughman. All the way through the poem Langland described the misery of the poor, and the selfishness and greed of the priests, monks and friars. He tried to teach that for all people, whether rich or poor, work and truth are the really important things in life.

Though the works of Chaucer and of Langland are so very different, they both tell us a great deal about the way in which people really lived in the fourteenth century, and what they thought about and what they looked like.

Another fourteenth-century writer who felt that the Church was not doing the good work it should do in the world was John Wyclif. He was very different from Langland. He was a Yorkshireman and was educated at the University of Oxford. He became a very learned man indeed and Master of Balliol College, Oxford. But he, too, felt that the clergy and the monks were too rich and worldly, and that the friars were no longer the poor teachers they had been at first, but were lazy and greedy. He felt that the Pope should not have the power to give high positions in the Church of England to foreign priests who did not understand or care for the English people, and neither should he have the power, as he had, to take large sums of money out of England, which should be spent on helping the poor.

A great many people agreed with Wyclif. They were called 'lollards' by the Churchmen, who opposed them—a word which means 'babblers'.

At first Wyclif wrote in Latin, but he is important in our story of the book because he suddenly decided to write in the language of the common people, in English. He began to write leaflets in simple plain language that ordinary people could understand. In them he denounced pilgrimages to the shrines of saints, the worship of images, the buying of pardons, and all kinds of other things that the Church supported. He said that the Bible itself should be the foundation of Christian faith, and that every man should be allowed to study the Bible for himself.

But the Bible was in Latin, which ordinary people could not read. So Wyclif set to work to translate it into English. Although Wyclif's translation is not the one we use now, the way in which he used the English language in that first English Bible has had a very great influence on our literature. That is why Wyclif is sometimes called the 'father of English prose', just as Chaucer is called the 'father of English poetry'.

While Chaucer and Langland and Wyclif and many others whose names have come down to us were writing both poetry and prose, others whose names we do not know were writing stories in verse that we now call ballads. The stories were usually about popular heroes, such as Robin Hood. Often the ballads must have been passed on from singer to singer, and probably they changed quite a lot from their original form. Sometimes the earliest written copy of a ballad that we have is quite late, though the ballad itself had been known and sung for generations.

Chevy Chase and *The Nut Brown Maid* are two of the earliest ballads we know. *Chevy Chase* is the story of a struggle between Percy of Northumberland and Douglas of Scotland early in the fifteenth century. *The Nut Brown Maid* is the story of a baron's daughter whose lover tells her he must fly to the forest and become an outlaw. She insists on following him, only to find in the end that what he had told her was only to test her love. He is really a great lord and on marrying him she becomes Countess of Westmorland.

Besides the ballads there were other longer stories, some of which have come down to us, though others may have been completely forgotten. They were usually in verse, and were probably recited by bards and ministrels in the great halls of manor houses and castles for generations, both in Normandy before the Norman Conquest, and afterwards in England. At first they were in Norman-French, which was one of the family of languages which had developed from

Latin—the language of the Romans. Such languages are called 'Romance' languages, and the stories, because they were in these languages, were called 'romances'.

From the thirteenth century onwards the romances were translated into English, and they were very popular for hundreds of years. They were usually about the amazing adventures of a young knight—his travels, his attempts to win his lady, the giants and dragons he killed, the dungeons and towers in which he was imprisoned, and so on. One of the best known of these stories was about a knight called Guy of Warwick, and another of the heroes was named Bevis of Southampton.

But whether the poems and stories and other writings of the Middle Ages were the work of great poets such as Chaucer, or great thinkers and reformers such as Wyclif, or of minstrels who sang to amuse the ordinary people of the time, they had one thing in common. If people were to read them they had to be written down by hand and patiently copied again and again by scribes who, as we have seen, often found their work very tedious.

CHAPTER XI

★

Forgotten Books Brought to Light Again

As you have seen, all through the Middle Ages there were a few people here and there who took a keen interest in books and in learning, and many monasteries and churches had collections of books. But more often than not the books that were copied and re-copied in the monasteries were those dealing with the Christian religion. The learning and literature of Greece and Rome was forgotten, and the books which had survived from earlier ages were neglected.

Then in the fourteenth and fifteenth centuries, in Italy, there came a great revival of interest in the art, literature, architecture and learning of the past. We call this revival the Renaissance, or re-birth of learning. People began to study all that was left of Greek and Roman sculpture and the ruins of the great architecture of the past, and to hunt for and read all they could find of the ancient manuscripts.

One of the earliest students who collected manuscripts of Ancient Greece and Rome was an Italian poet named Petrarch. He lived from 1304 to 1374. When he was a young man he studied to be a lawyer at Bologna, but instead of working as he should have done he spent all his time collecting and reading the works of the ancient Roman writers. His father was so angry that he burnt most of his books, only sparing some of the works of Virgil and Cicero because Petrarch begged him so hard not to destroy them.

All his life Petrarch went on collecting ancient books. He would go on long journeys himself or would send messengers right across Europe to places where he heard ancient manuscripts were to be found.

Another famous collector was a writer named Boccaccio. He, too, travelled about looking for any fragments he could find of the work of the ancient authors. There is a description in existence of a visit he paid to Monte Cassino—the monastery St. Benedict had founded in Italy. The Monte Cassino library had been very famous, as the monks had not only made copies of books by Christian authors, but had also copied many by Terence, Virgil, Horace, Homer, Seneca, and other Greek and Roman writers. But, unfortunately, by the fourteenth century the monastery was not what it had been in the past, and Boccaccio found the library in a terrible state. There was no door to the room in which the precious books were kept, and the books themselves, and the benches and desks, were thick with dust. But, worse still, some of the books had been cut to pieces, and separate pages had been sold to boys for a few pence. Boccaccio was very distressed that work which had been done with such care and patience should be so neglected.

Monte Cassino was not, of course, the only monastery in which the precious books written centuries earlier were no longer cared for. At a time when people outside the monasteries were becoming more enthusiastic about books and learning than they had been for centuries, the monks inside the monasteries were often ignorant and quite unfit to have charge of their precious possessions.

Another famous collector of the fifteenth century, named Poggio Bracciolini, described a visit he paid to the monastery of St. Gall, where, among a large number of books, he found one called the 'Institutions' of Quintillian, which up to that time was only known through one incomplete copy which Petrarch had found. Poggio says the book was covered with dust and filthy with neglect and age, and that the books were housed in a 'most foul and obscene dungeon at the very bottom of a tower, a place into which condemned criminals would hardly have been thrust'.

Of Poggio we are told that 'no severity of winter cold, no snow, no length of journey, no roughness of roads, prevented him from bringing the monuments of literature to light'.

Fortunately, as the monks no longer valued their books, they usually had no objection to selling them to men who did, and who took care to see that they were properly looked after.

Other book collectors visited the neglected libraries of Monte Cassino and other monasteries and rescued some of the valuable books. The Popes, and many members of the great and wealthy families of Rome, Florence, Venice and other cities of Italy at this time spent immense fortunes in searching for and buying copies of books by Greek and Roman writers—the classics, as we call them. Some of them went to Constantinople and the monasteries of the East, and returned laden with manuscripts. They were tremendously excited if they happened to find a copy of a work of which no copy existed in the West, so far as anyone knew. The head of a great banking firm, Cosimo de' Medici, was one of these enthusiastic collectors, and he told his agents to buy every manuscript they could lay their hands on, regardless of expense.

Italian students, too, flocked to Constantinople in order to study Greek so that they could read Greek books, and when possible buy Greek manuscripts to take back to Italy with them.

It is lucky that all this happened during the fourteenth and early fifteenth centuries, for in May 1453 Constantinople was captured by the Turks. The Italian students and many learned Greeks fled to Italy, carrying as many of their prized manuscripts as they could. These people and their books helped to spread the learning of Ancient Greece over Italy and then over the rest of Europe.

The books collected by wealthy Italians at the time of the Renaissance formed libraries, some of which have gone on growing and still exist. There is the great Vatican Library, for instance, in the Pope's palace in Rome; and the Laurentian Library in Florence which was made up originally of books collected by Cosimo de' Medici and members of his family. And there are many others.

Some of the libraries started by enthusiastic scholars of the Renaissance have had their ups and downs. Petrarch, for instance, gave a large number of books to the city of Venice for a public library on condition that they were not to be divided or sold. But years later the people who should have looked after them ceased to trouble about them, and most of the books got lost or were stolen. In 1635 a number of them were found lying forgotten in an upper room and so ruined by damp that they had become shapeless and useless lumps.

It is not only through neglect that precious books have sometimes been lost. There have always, from time to time, been people who have taken a delight in destroying books they did not approve of or understand. Such people have not always been ignorant barbarians, such as those who destroyed the libraries of Ancient Rome. In Florence, for instance, in the fifteenth century, a Dominican friar and preacher named Savonarola hated the new ideas and the new learning that were spreading everywhere through the study of classical literature. He became very powerful for a time. He tried to put a stop to all frivolity and vanity, and in the public square in Florence he made a great 'bonfire of vanities' on which he urged people to fling their costly ornaments and jewels. And from the great library of books the Medici family had collected, and which at that time belonged to the Dominicans, Savonarola and his followers took some of the most richly illuminated and bound volumes of the works of Petrarch, Boccaccio and other writers and flung them on the bonfire.

The Medici collection of books later formed part of a public library in Florence, and the great painter and sculptor Michelangelo designed the building in which it was housed, and the desks on which the books rested.

Libraries in the Middle Ages and at the time of the Renaissance, did not look in the least like our present-day libraries. The books did not stand upright on shelves round the walls as they usually do now, or even in separate bookcases standing out in the room. As you read in Chapter VII, they were kept in chests or cupboards. But there was another way in which special books were sometimes kept in early times. They were often placed on a sloping desk, and a chain was fastened through a piece of metal attached to the cover of the book and was secured to the desk. The chain was long enough for the book to be opened and read, but no one could take it away. Such a reading-desk sometimes stood in the church attached to a monastery.

When monasteries, colleges and such places began putting their books all together in a special room, they used this same method. A number of reading desks, or lecterns, were put at intervals down each side of the room, at right angles to the wall, so that they got plenty of light from the windows. The lecterns might be long enough to hold several books, and a chain was fixed to the cover of each book, the other end being attached to a rod that ran along the top of the lectern.

Sometimes the lecterns would be so high that readers had to stand at them. Perhaps this was so that they would have no temptation to fall asleep over their studies. European students could not do what Chinese students were told to do in an ancient Chinese book—tie their pigtails to a beam so that if they drowsed and their heads fell forward the pull would awaken them.

More often the lecterns were lower, and each one had a bench in front of it on which the reader sat. Later there was

Lecterns in a medieval library

sometimes a shelf below the level of the desk, on which other books could be kept, each one being chained to a staple.

Then at last men began to stand books up on end, side by side on shelves above the desk. At first there were only two shelves; then the 'presses', as they were called, were made higher, and there were three or even four shelves above the desk, and perhaps one below. But the presses still stood at right angles to the walls, between the windows, so that they formed a number of three-sided rooms, or stalls, down the length of the library with a passage between. Each stall had its bench on which the readers could sit when studying the books, and each book was fastened firmly by its chain to the rod that was fixed above or below each shelf. This meant that the books had to be put into the shelves the wrong way round, with the spine (the narrow part on which the title appears) facing inwards out of sight, as the chain was fastened to the front edge of the binding.

We can see how odd this looked if we visit, or see a photograph of, the chained library at Hereford Cathedral, which has been arranged just as it was in the Middle Ages.

The revival of interest in classical art, architecture, literature and learning that started in Italy gradually spread over the rest of Europe. But it did not have very much effect on England until the sixteenth century, and by that time something very important indeed had happened. Printing had been invented—the art that was to make books plentiful and so spread the new learning more than anything else could have done, and that was soon going to make the work of the patient scribes no longer necessary.

CHAPTER XII

★

Paper and Printing

For the thousand years during which the beautiful illuminated manuscripts you read about in Chapters VIII and IX were being produced, the material on which books were written, you remember, was parchment or vellum. But about the middle of the twelfth century Europeans learnt for the first time about another material— one that in time was to take the place of animal skins altogether, though not for nearly three hundred years. This, of course, was paper.

It is a very surprising thing that paper was made in China over a thousand years before anyone in Europe knew anything about it. The ancient Chinese were very remarkable people. They learnt and invented many things that were unknown in the West, but travel was so slow and difficult, and the East and West were so completely separated from each other, that ideas and new discoveries took centuries to pass from one country to another.

An old record tells us that the first paper was made in China by a courtier named Tsai-Lun about A.D. 105. Proof that paper existed in China very early indeed was found by an Englishman in 1907. He found an ancient sealed bin attached to a watchtower of the Great Wall of China, and in it were a number of ancient documents. Some were written on wood and some on silk, but among them were nine letters written on *paper*. By the script in which they were written it was possible to prove that they were not later than A.D. 137—about thirty years after the date given for Tsai-Lun's invention.

You can see one of these letters, on the oldest piece of paper in the world, in the British Museum.

Although paper was used all over China, and had replaced other materials by the fifth century, it was not until three hundred years later that it reached even as far as the city of Baghdad. The Mohammedans (Mohammed lived from about A.D. 570 to A.D. 632) knew about paper and used it freely, but as they had closed the trade routes between Europe and the East, it was not until the twelfth century that the new invention—only by now it was not very new—was introduced into Spain by the Moors.

The word paper is a form of the word papyrus. Papyrus was still well known in the days when paper first arrived in the Near East, and the new material, which looked something like it, was called by the same name.

Europeans did not accept paper with enthusiasm immediately it was introduced into Spain. The Moors were hated and feared, and Christians distrusted paper because it was used by people they regarded as heathens. So it was not until 1270 that men began to make paper in Italy, at Fabriano, and not until the fourteenth century that they began to make it in France and Germany. The first paper mill in England that we know anything about was set up in Hertford early in the sixteenth century by a man named John Tate. But paper had been used in England for two hundred years, since 1309, so it must have been imported, probably from Spain.

For a long time all paper was made by hand. Rags were soaked in water and then beaten until all the fibres were separated and the liquid was like a kind of thick milk. Then the workman took a wooden frame which enclosed a mesh or screen made of copper wire. Over it he fitted another frame, called a deckle. He dipped the frame into the tub of liquid and drew it out, giving it a little circular shake so that the fibres would fall in all directions. The water drained away through the wire screen, leaving the fibres behind in a flat sheet, which, when it had been placed between felts and pressed in a hand-press, and dried, became a sheet of paper.

Where the liquid oozed out from under the deckle it left a feathery edge to the paper, which is called the deckle-edge. A deckle-edge is characteristic of hand-made paper.

You can see, can't you, that paper could not be made very quickly by this method? But parchment took even longer to prepare, and cost more. Paper, too, was lighter, and if it was well made of good material, it could be nearly as strong as parchment. So gradually paper was used more and more.

Then in the fifteenth century came the invention that made it possible for books to be made in greater numbers than had ever been possible before, and large quantities of paper became absolutely necessary.

We say that printing was invented in the fifteenth century but we really mean that a certain kind of printing—printing with movable types, which I will explain later—was invented at that time. Men had known how to *print* for centuries before that.

I expect you have made lino-cuts or potato-cuts at school, so you know what printing is. In the simplest kind of printing, a shape is drawn on the flat surface of the piece of lino or wood or whatever is being used. Then the background is cut away, leaving the pattern or shape raised. The block is then inked and a piece of paper, or some similar material, is pressed over it (or the block, if it is small enough, is pressed down on the paper). In this way the pattern is transferred in ink, or printed, on to the paper.

This kind of printing—block printing as it is called—was known in England as early as William the Conqueror's time. Kings had their monograms cut in wood or metal and stamped on their charters. But as with paper, so with printing. The Chinese knew about it long before anyone in Europe.

Old records tell us that in the second century A.D. certain important Chinese books were cut on stone tablets and were set up outside the university, so that people could take impressions from them. Then from the sixth century the Chinese were printing pictures, such as portraits of Buddha,

A wood block

from wooden blocks, and whole pages of Chinese symbols or words. And we know that right back in the ninth century, in the days when the Danes were raiding Britain, the Chinese printed a book that is the earliest of all known printed books.

Its story is a very romantic one. In China, near the border of Turkestan, there is a great cliff in the face of which a number of caves have been cut. For hundreds of years, from about

A.D. 366, Chinese holy men, or monks, lived in these caves, which are called 'The Caves of the Thousand Buddhas'. Early in the eleventh century they walled up a number of sacred and valuable treasures in one of the caves in order to keep them safe. There the treasures remained undisturbed for nine hundred years, until, about the year 1900, a priest who was restoring a painting on a wall in one of the caves discovered that the wall was of brick instead of stone. Behind the brick wall was the secret chamber and in it were thousands of manuscript rolls dating from the fourth to the tenth centuries—and this one block-printed book.

The block-printed book is in the form of a roll, too, and is made up of seven sheets of paper. Altogether it is about twelve inches wide by sixteen feet long. At the beginning is a picture of a god, sitting on a throne and talking to an old man who is kneeling before him, while a large number of Buddhist monks and attendants stand around. An inscription tells us that the book was printed by Wang Chieh 'for free and general distribution, in order, in deep reverence, to perpetuate the memory of his parents'. Each section of the book is printed from one solid block, on which the Chinese symbols were cut. It was printed in A.D. 868.

The Chinese continued to print block books, and in the tenth century, by order of the Emperor, all the works of the writer Confucius were cut on wooden blocks and printed. The work took twenty-one years, and when it was completed there were one hundred and thirty volumes, or rolls.

Block-printing was used in Europe from the fourteenth century for making playing-cards, and for printing little religious pictures which pilgrims liked to buy. One with the date 1423 printed on it was found pasted inside the binding of an old book. This is the earliest one of which we know the exact date. It shows St. Christopher carrying the child Jesus across a river. There are some very queer trees and huts, a water-

A Page from the Biblia Pauperum, or Poor Man's Bible

mill, a man with a donkey and another carrying a sack, and an animal that is presumably a rabbit, poking its head out of a hole.

In making such blocks as this all the background was cut away, leaving the lines of the drawing raised. Then the engraver dabbed ink on the surface of the block with a pad, put a piece of paper over the block and rubbed the back of the paper with a burnisher, or ran a roller, called a frotton, over it. Then he removed the paper, with the picture printed on it, and put it aside to dry.

The printed outline drawing was often coloured by hand. The St. Christopher print that was found inside an old book was coloured in this way. St. Christopher's robe is red, and the lining and haloes are yellow. The robes of Jesus and of a hermit and of the water are blue, the grass and the leaves are bright green, and the faces and limbs are pale flesh-colour. Underneath the picture is an inscription in Latin. Translated into English it says:

> *On whatever day the face of Christopher thou shalt see,*
> *On that day no evil form of death shall visit thee.*

There are one or two similar pictures in existence, which some people believe were printed even earlier.

Soon people in Europe realized, as they had done in China centuries earlier, that if they could print single pictures from wood blocks, they could also print a series of pages, join them together, and so make a book. In Europe men began to make block-books, as they are called, early in the fifteenth century.

The most popular of the block-books was called Biblia Pauperum, or The Poor Man's Bible. It consisted of a number of pictures of the most important events in the Old and the New Testaments, with a few words describing and explaining the picture.

Paper and Printing

One of the block-books was a Latin grammar from which little boys studied in the schools of the fifteenth century.

If you have ever done any lino- or wood-cutting you will realize what a tedious and slow job the printing of such a book must have been, when every page had to be carved out completely on a single block of wood, pictures and words as well.

Sooner or later, of course, someone was bound to realize that instead of having one big block for each page of a book it was possible to have hundreds of little blocks, each one having one letter of the alphabet only carved on it, and that the blocks could be arranged and rearranged to form any words or sentences required.

Here again the Chinese were ahead of us. Some time between 1041 and 1049 a Chinese named Pi Sheng got the idea of moulding the different characters in which the Chinese language is written in clay, baking the clay hard, and so forming types that could be arranged in a frame and printed from. But the method was not practised very generally in China, perhaps because in writing Chinese thousands of different characters were needed, which made the whole process a very difficult one. The language could not be written with twenty-six simple letters, as the languages of Europe can.

The question is—who was the first European to cut those letters on separate blocks, and so make type?

CHAPTER XIII

★

Who Invented Printing?

Most people believe that printing was invented by a German named Johann Gutenberg. He was born at Mainz about the year 1400. Later he was living in Strasburg, and there he made an agreement with a number of people that he would teach them certain 'secret arts'. What were those 'secret arts'? No one knows for certain, but it is believed that they may have been the arts of making 'type', or separate letters carved in wood or cast in metal, and printing from them. There are in existence three tiny fragments of three different books which many people believe were printed in Strasburg between 1444 and 1448 by Gutenberg, and which are almost certainly the oldest pieces of printing in existence.

One thing that is certain is that by 1450 Gutenberg had returned to Mainz. There a wealthy goldsmith named Johann Fust provided the money so that Gutenberg could set up as a printer. But poor Gutenberg was always in trouble over money, and when in 1455 Fust brought an action against Gutenberg and demanded his money back Gutenberg was unable to pay. So his printing office and all that was in it became the property of Fust.

The next year, 1456, there appeared the book that is the earliest complete book printed in Europe with movable types that has come down to us. It was a splendid two-volume Bible. It is called the Gutenberg Bible because it must have been the book on which Gutenberg was working during the five years before his printing office was handed over to Fust.

Sometimes you may hear it called the Mazarin Bible. Mazarin was a cardinal and minister of France in the days of Louis XIII and Louis XIV, and died in 1661. He left a very fine library, and about the middle of the eighteenth century a student who was working among the books noticed a very early printed Bible in two volumes. It was Gutenberg's Bible, of course, but a very important and interesting thing about it was a note that was written at the back. The note said that on 15th August 1456 a vicar of a church at Mainz named Heinrich Cremer had finished painting in the initials in that particular copy, and binding it. This proved that the book must have been printed before that date.

Another interesting thing about the Mazarin copy is that it has forty-two lines to the page, whereas some other copies of Gutenberg's Bible have forty or forty-one lines only on some of the early pages, and forty-two on the rest. This shows that the printers must have experimented a little at first before they decided that forty-two lines looked best, and the Bible in the Mazarin library must have been a second edition printed after the type had been made up again with forty-two lines all the way through.

There is no printer's name on any copy of the Gutenberg Bible, or any date except the one written in by Cremer in the Mazarin copy. In fact there is not a single book in existence that bears Gutenberg's name, and it is only by examining ancient legal documents, agreements, court records and so on that experts have discovered what little we know about him, and have decided that he was the man to whom the credit for inventing this wonderful new art should be given.

Whether Gutenberg did actually invent the art of printing

from movable types or not, there is no doubt whatever that it was his skill and knowledge and hard work that produced the wonderful Bible that bears his name. About three hundred copies of the Bible were printed. There are still about forty copies known to exist, and it is one of the world's most valuable books. A copy was sold to America a little while ago for over £37,000.

But there are some people who believe that the art of printing from movable types was invented at Haarlem in Holland by a man named Laurens Janszoon. He was sexton at the parish church at Haarlem, so he is usually called Coster, which is the Dutch word for sexton. According to the story Coster cut some letters out of the bark of a tree and printed from them in order to amuse his grandchildren. Then he made some better types, first in wood and later cast in lead, and prepared some wood-cut pictures and printed a book which was called *The Mirror of Our Salvation*. It had pictures at the top of each page and a description below, something like the 'Poor Man's Bible'. We are told that this book appeared in 1441—fifteen years before Gutenberg's Bible—but if so not a single copy has survived and there is no proof that it ever really existed.

The story goes on that Coster set up in business as a printer and engaged some assistants, one of whom ran away and took the secret to Mainz.

One difficulty about this story is that it was not written down until 1568, well over a hundred years after Coster is said to have invented printing, and during the hundred years there is no mention anywhere either of his name or of his invention. It is impossible to say whether there is any truth in the story or not. But not long ago, inside the binding of some very old books, some fragments of early printed work were discovered which some people believe were done by Coster.

Some day, perhaps, something will be found that will settle the problem once and for all.

Whoever it was who invented movable types, he and those who followed him had a great many problems to settle. The earliest printers probably first drew each letter of the alpha-

An early printing press

bet, wrong way round, on the top of a little block of wood. All the little blocks would have to be exactly the same height. Then they had to cut away the background so that the letter stood up plainly. It was no use, of course, cutting one copy only of each letter. To print only a few pages of a book some hundreds of copies of each letter would be needed, and each one would have to be cut by hand. This would be very slow, and very soon printers learnt to make a mould the shape of each letter. Molten metal was poured into the mould, and when it was set and hard it was taken out of the mould and there was a letter the exact shape and size of the original wooden letter, but in metal. As many letters as were necessary could be made from the original mould.

The first printers had to learn how to arrange their letters, or types, so that they would make lines all exactly the same length, and how to fasten the types firmly together so that they would not shift when being printed. And they had to experiment with inks until they found the kind that would serve them best, and design their own printing presses.

In the early days no printer had enough copies of each letter to print a whole book. A few pages would be set up, a number of copies printed, then the types would be separated and cleaned and a few more pages would be set up. And so on until the book was finished.

But to return to Mainz. Johann Fust carried on Gutenberg's printing works with a young man named Schoeffer, who had worked with Gutenberg. In 1457 they issued a Psalter which is the very first printed book that gives us definite information about itself. There is an inscription at the back which, translated, says: 'The present copy of the Psalms, adorned with beauty of capital letters, and sufficiently marked out with rubrics, has been thus fashioned by an ingenious invention of printing and stamping without any driving of the pen, and to the worship of God has been diligently brought to completion by Johann Fust, a citizen of Mainz, and Peter Schoeffer of Gernsheim, in the year of the Lord 1457, on the vigil of the Feast of the Assumption.'

You notice that the inscription mentions that the book is 'adorned with beauty of capital letters and sufficiently marked

out with rubrics'. You see, the whole idea of the early printers was to make their printed books look as exactly like illuminated manuscripts as they possibly could. They cut their
type letters to look just like the written letters of the time, and
as at that time, in Germany, the Gothic style of letter was
being used, it is in that style that these first printed books
appeared. Very often, at first, spaces were left to be filled in
by the illuminators and the rubricators, just as they had been
in the hand-written books.

But one of the amazing things about the Psalter printed by
Fust and Schoeffer is that the initials and ornamental letters
were not done by hand but were printed in three colours, and
were so beautifully done that they still astonish everyone who
sees them.

Of course, as soon as the first printed books had appeared
other men began to practise the new art. Before long there
were several printing works in Mainz. But in 1462 fighting
broke out and Mainz was sacked. Many craftsmen left the
town and settled in other parts of Germany. Towns such as
Augsburg, Nuremberg, Cologne, and Strasburg became
famous centres for printing.

From Germany the art of printing spread to other countries. In Italy the very first printing press was set up in a
monastery in a town called Subiaco, about thirty miles from
Rome, by two Germans called Sweynheym and Pannartz.
Soon printing spread to Rome, and later to Venice, which
soon became the greatest printing centre in Europe.

The first printer to set up a press in Venice was John of
Spires, and the second, in 1470, was a Frenchman named
Nicolas Jenson. He had been master of the Mint at Tours
when rumours began to reach France about a wonderful new
way of producing books. King Charles II of France sent
Jenson to Mainz to find out all about the new art. But by the
time he had mastered it Charles II had died, and Jenson

did not think the new king, Louis XI, would be interested. So instead of returning to France he went to Venice.

Jenson is famous for the types he designed, which were based on the best hand-lettering of Italy. You remember the first printers imitated the Gothic handwriting popular in Germany. But the Italians did not care for the Gothic script. The scholars in Italy who had for so long been keenly interested in the art and learning of ancient Greece and Rome, had developed a style of handwriting based on the clearer, rounder writing of earlier centuries. We call the Italian types Jenson and his followers designed 'Roman', but they called them 'antiqua'.

Before long there were over two hundred printing establishments in Venice, and books of all kinds were being printed. But the most famous of all the Venetian printers was a great scholar named Aldus Manutius (usually known simply as Aldus). Many of the earliest printed books were large and were very elaborately decorated. They were very expensive and could only be bought by wealthy people. Aldus was the first printer to produce small, cheap books that could be bought by students who had not much money to spend. He was a master of Greek language and literature, and he had a fount of Greek type designed and cut so that he could print books in Greek.

He also designed a new Roman type which slanted as handwriting usually does, and which took up less space than the other types, although it was no less clear to read. This slanting type is still used, and we call it 'italic'. We only use it now for special purposes, such as for printing foreign words in an English book, but Aldus printed whole books in it.

Aldus used in his books a sign, or printer's mark, by means of which people could tell that he was the printer. It was an anchor with a dolphin twined round its stem. We are told that the dolphin stood for speed and the anchor for firmness.

Aldus was a very energetic and busy man, and he hated being disturbed by people with nothing better to do than waste his time. So he had a notice put on his door which said:

'Whoever thou art thou art earnestly requested by Aldus to state thy business briefly and to take thy departure promptly. In this way thou mayest be of service, even as was Hercules to the weary Atlas. For this is a place of work for all who may enter.'

A tooled leather binding

Aldus was one of the first printers to use a new process called 'gold tooling' on the bindings of his books. The first printed books were bound just as the earlier manuscript books had been, with oak boards covered with leather, and sometimes fitted with metal corners or other ornaments, and with strong metal clasps to fasten them. But another way of decorating books had been practised too. A pattern had been made on the surface of the books by pressing hot tools made

I   129

of brass into the leather. The tools would be cut into different shapes and patterns, such as flowers, coats of arms, monograms, geometric designs, ornamental rules, and letters of the alphabet. Towards the end of the fifteenth century a way of making the patterns in gold was discovered. The same tools were used, and the pattern was first stamped in as usual. Then thin sheets of gold were placed over the pattern and the hot tools were pressed on to the surface of the book again. The gold stuck on to the leather wherever the hot tool had pressed.

During the sixteenth century the raised patterns and inset precious stones that had been used in earlier days were gradually given up altogether, and books for the first time were made to stand up side by side on a shelf instead of lying flat one on top of another as they had always done before. Then, in time, it became usual to stamp the title on the narrow back of the book—the 'spine'—in gold letters.

By the year 1500—forty-four years after Gutenberg's Bible appeared—printing had spread over almost the whole of Europe, and teachers, students, lawyers, churchmen and people everywhere must have wondered how men had ever managed without it. But everyone was not pleased, of course. The scribes saw that the printing press was going to destroy their way of earning a living, and they hated it. The illuminators and rubricators did not suffer so much at first, but in time they, too, were not needed, as printers no longer had their printed books illuminated by hand.

At first some people despised printed books as being far inferior to hand-written ones. A famous scribe called Vespasiano da Bisticci was agent for Frederick, Duke of Urbino, in the fifteenth century. The Duke was one of the enthusiastic collectors of ancient books and had a very famous library. Vespasiano tells us that thirty to forty copyists were busy for fourteen years copying ancient Greek and Latin manuscripts and the works of the Italian poets and the religious writers of earlier days. The books were beautifully illuminated and were bound in crimson leather with silver clasps—'nor', says Vespasiano, 'could you find a single printed volume in the whole library for the Duke would have been ashamed to own one'.

But in spite of all opposition printing had come to stay.

Early printed books are now valued very highly and collectors will pay large sums for rare copies. Books printed before the year 1500 are called 'incunabula', which means 'cradle' books, or books printed when the art of printing was in its infancy.

CHAPTER XIV

★

Printing Reaches England

J ust twenty years after Gutenberg's Bible appeared in
Mainz William Caxton set up a printing press in a
house that had been part of the Almonry of Westminster Abbey, in London. The next year he produced the
very first book to be printed in England. It was called *The
Dictes and Sayinges of the Philosophers.*

But although this was the first book printed in England,
it was not the first to be printed in the English language.
Books in English had already been printed by Caxton in
Flanders.

William Caxton was born in Kent, and when he was about
fifteen or sixteen years old he was apprenticed to a mercer, or
dealer in woollen goods in London. When his master died
Caxton went to Bruges, in Flanders, which was a very important port in those days, and a centre of the wool trade. A
great many English wool and cloth merchants lived there.

Caxton was very successful, and in 1462 he became Gover-
nor of all the English merchants in the Netherlands. Some
years later the Duke of Burgundy married Princess Margaret,
who was the sister of the King of England, King Edward IV.
The new Duchess persuaded Caxton to give up being a
mercer and to enter her service.

Caxton was well educated and very much interested in books. With the encouragement of the Duchess he translated into English a book about Troy that had already been translated into French from Latin. Then, so that copies of the book could be supplied quickly to all the people who wanted it, he learned the new art of printing, probably in Cologne, and set up his own printing press in Bruges. Here, about 1474, he printed the very first book to be printed in English, *The Recuyell* (gathering together) *of the Hystoryes of Troye.*

Not many copies of this book survive, but one that is in a library in California is particularly interesting because in it there is a full-page picture showing Caxton presenting the book to the Duchess of Burgundy. He is kneeling on the tiled floor, holding up the two volumes of the book to the Duchess, who is wearing the very long dress of the time heaped in folds all round her feet. On her head is a head-dress with a long tapering spire rising behind it, from which a long veil hangs. All around stand her ladies, dressed in the same way. This particular copy of *The Recuyell of the Hystoryes of Troye* once belonged to Edward IV's wife, Elizabeth Woodville, who was the mother of the two little princes who were murdered in the Tower of London.

Caxton printed a book called *The Game and Playe of the Chesse* while he was still in Bruges, and one or two other works. Then, after being away over thirty years he returned to England and opened his printing establishment in Westminster.

In those days the House of Commons met in the Chapter House of Westminster Abbey, so Caxton may have chosen to be near it so that the Members could see his books, when he displayed them on a stall outside his house.

In Caxton's time most traders had a sign outside their houses of business. Caxton's sign was a white shield with a vertical stripe up the centre in red. In heraldry such a stripe is called a 'pale', so Caxton's printing establishment was at 'The Sign of the Red Pale'.

The first book Caxton printed in England—*The Dictes and Sayinges of the Philosophers*—appeared in 1477. During the next fifteen years Caxton printed ninety-six different books dealing with all kinds of subjects. Like many of the early printers Caxton was a man of education who loved books and who took up printing because he saw that it was a way of spreading learning and of putting books into the hands of everyone who wanted them.

He loved the work of Geoffrey Chaucer, whom he called 'that worshipful man' who 'ought eternally to be remembered', so he printed copies of *The Canterbury Tales*. He also printed the works of other early English poets, and romances such as the *Morte d'Arthur*, which, you remember, was all about King Arthur and his knights. Then there was history. There were not many history books in existence in Caxton's time, but such as there were he printed, including one called the *Polychronicon*, which had been written by a monk named Ralph Higden, who died in 1363. Caxton brought it up to his own date himself. One of Caxton's books told people how to behave and was called *The Boke of Good Manners*. He also translated no less than twenty-two books into English from other languages, so that they could be printed in the language of the people who wanted to read them.

But here Caxton came up against a difficulty. The English language was not so settled as it is now, and it was still changing. 'Our language now used varieth far from that which was used and spoken when I was born,' Caxton wrote. And it varied so much from one district to another that men from different parts of the country could not understand each other. Caxton writes: '. . . . in my days happened that certain merchants were in a ship in Thames for to have sailed over the sea to Zealand, and for lack of wind they tarried at Foreland, and went on land to refresh them. And one of them, named Sheffield, a mercer, came into a house and asked for meat, and especially he asked them after eggs. And the good wife answered that she could speak no French, and the merchant was angry, for he also could speak no French, but would have had eggs, but she understood him not. And then at last another said he would have eyren, then the good wife said she understood him well. Lo! what should a man in these days now write, eggs or eyren? Certainly it is hard to please every man by cause of diversity and change of language.'

Other books that Caxton printed were service books for use in churches and monasteries, and religious works such as the *Golden Legend*, the thirteenth-century book, you remember, of stories and legends about the saints. It was a very long book—four hundred and forty-three leaves in the French printed edition—and it is no wonder that Caxton, who did the greater part of the translation into English himself, wrote that he was 'half desperate to have accomplisht it' and ready to 'lay it apart'. But Caxton was encouraged and helped in his work by all kinds of important people, including Kings Edward IV, Richard III, and Henry VII, and various Dukes, Duchesses, Archbishops, and others. The Earl of Arundel begged him to go on with the *Golden Legend*, and promised him a yearly fee of a buck in summer and a doe in winter when it was done.

The *Golden Legend* was illustrated with seventy woodcut pictures, but a great many of Caxton's books had no pictures at all.

Where we should put a comma or full stop in a book, Caxton printed a short upright line.

There are two unusual things about the introduction of printing into England. England is the only country in Europe in which the new art was introduced by a native instead of by someone from a foreign land, and it is the only country in which the first book to be printed was in the language of the country itself. Nearly everywhere else the first book was a Bible, or Psalter, or some other book connected with the Church or religion, and written in Latin.

Caxton had no sons, so after his death his business was carried on by a man named Wynkyn de Worde who had been one of his apprentices.

De Worde stayed at the 'Sign of the Red Pale' for some years, then he moved to a house in Fleet Street, where his sign was a sun. Fleet Street and the district round St. Paul's Cathedral had already become a centre of the book and printing trade, because by this time a great many foreigners had settled there. Some of them imported unbound printed books from abroad and bound and sold them in England. They were called stationers, though some of them were printers as well.

It is an interesting thing that now, after four hundred and fifty years, Fleet Street in London is still a great printing centre, though the things that are printed are mainly newspapers and magazines such as Caxton and Wynkyn de Worde could hardly have imagined.

Almost opposite to Wynkyn de Worde in Fleet Street, at the 'Sign of the George' next to St. Dunstan's Church, lived another famous early printer, Richard Pynson. He printed one of the first books which attempted to help English people visiting France to speak and understand French; also a Latin-English Dictionary, and a cookery book 'for a pryncis household'. In those days feasts were sometimes given which lasted many days, and in which, Pynson tells us, as many as 8,590 animals of all kinds were used, not to speak of vast numbers of birds, fish, pastries and jellies.

Pynson was made King's Printer, or, in the words of the time, 'printer unto the Kynges Most Noble Grace' in 1509, when Henry VIII became king. It was he who printed a book for the king called *Assertio Septem Sacramentorum* (Assertion of the Seven Sacraments), which led to Henry VIII being given a title by the Pope which our kings have held ever since, 'Fidei Defensor', meaning 'Defender of the Faith'. You can see the letters F.D. stamped on all our coins.

The first books printed in England, as in other places, were in Gothic type. Pynson was the first English printer to use Roman type. Gradually Roman took the place of Gothic everywhere, except in Germany. In England Gothic type continued to be used for a long time for law books and for books used in churches, but Roman was used for everything else. In Germany people would not have anything to do with Roman type at all, and German books and newspapers are still often printed in Gothic type. Even as late as last century the German General Bismarck would not read a book if it was printed in Roman type.

In some other ways the first printed books continued for a long time to be like the old manuscript books. The scribes, in order to save time, and space on the paper, often shortened words—'abbreviated' them as we say. We still do this sometimes. We write Mr., for instance, instead of Mister, and No. instead of number (or numero). The scribes had used a great many abbreviations and the printers went on using them all for some time, but gradually most of them were dropped.

Another way in which the printed books were like the manuscript books was that they had no title-pages. One of the first English title-pages we know anything about was printed in 1527 by a printer in Southwark called Peter Treveris. The book was Higden's *Polychronicon*, of which you remember Caxton had also printed an edition. If you could see the title-page you would notice that the way in which the title is printed also illustrates how early printers followed in the footsteps of the scribes. In writing the scribes often joined two letters together to form 'ligatures', and the early printers did the same. On Treveris's title-page, in the word 'Poly-cronicon (which he, by the way, spelt without the h which is generally put in nowadays), the C and the R, and the C and the O are joined together.

By degrees printers gave up using most of the ligatures, but a few have survived. You sometimes see a and e joined, also o and e, and fi, fl and ff. But the commonest ligature still in use is the sign & for 'and', which we now call ampersand. Although it does not look like it now, this sign was originally a ligature made up of the letters e and t, 'et', meaning 'and' in Latin. This sign got its name 'ampersand' in rather a curious way. At one time it used to be put at the end of the alphabet, and in learning the alphabet the pupil said 'w, x, y, z and, per se, and'. 'Per se' means 'by itself'. Gradually the four words were run together and people forgot their original meaning and used the word 'ampersand' as the name of the sign.

Pynson died in 1535 and Wynkyn de Worde in 1540, and by that time printers and printing presses were to be found almost everywhere. Printing had even crossed the ocean to America, for in 1539 a German printer named Juan Crom-bergh, who was working in Spain, sent an Italian assistant of his over to Mexico City, where he set up the first printing press.

CHAPTER XV

★

Printers in Trouble

***

Printing had come just at the right moment to spread the learning and the new ideas that so many people were keenly interested in at the time of the Renaissance. But printers did not have things all their own way. Many of the new ideas that were spreading over Europe were hated by the Catholic Church. Before long printers found themselves in trouble if they printed anything which the Church did not approve of.

You remember how in the fourteenth century in England Wyclif had quarrelled with the Catholic Church and had written pamphlets against the Pope and the monks, and against many things the Church did which Wyclif thought were wrong. Nothing much came of his protests at the time, but early in the sixteenth century the German, Martin Luther, began saying very much the same things that Wyclif had said. He and his followers, who were called Protestants, believed, as Wyclif had done, that the Bible should be the basis of Christianity, and they pointed out that there is nothing in the Bible about the power of the Pope or of the Church. Soon there were thousands of Protestants all over Europe, especially in the North, and the Catholic Church was doing its best to suppress them. More and more people wanted to study the Bible for themselves.

139

The first Bibles that had been printed were copies of the Vulgate—the Bible in Latin that St. Jerome had translated from Hebrew and Greek originals in the fourth century. But about the time that printing was invented, in the middle of the fifteenth century, the Turks overran Constantinople, and scholars from the east of Europe fled to the west, bringing their learning and their ancient books with them. They helped to increase the tremendous interest that western scholars were already taking in the art and literature and knowledge of Ancient Greece and Rome. Some of these scholars studied manuscript copies of the Bible in Greek, and realized that they were different in some ways from the Vulgate, or Latin Bible, they had always known.

In Geneva a printer named Froben got the famous scholar Erasmus to prepare a Greek New Testament from Greek manuscripts, and it was printed in 1516. A few years later a complete Greek Bible that had been prepared in the University of Alcala appeared. It was called a Polyglot (or many language) Bible, because Latin and Hebrew texts appeared side by side with the Greek in the Old Testament, and Latin with the Greek in the New Testament. The Church did not approve of any 'interference', as it called it, with the Latin Bible which had come down to it from Jerome.

A printer in Paris, called Robert Estienne, divided the New Testament into verses because he thought it would be easier for people to read. The Church was furious with him, but Estienne happened to be in great favour with the king, Francis I. The king accepted a copy of the book when it was printed, and that made it possible for it to be offered for sale. But the Churchmen refused to use it, or to allow it to be used in the university.

After his protector, Francis I, had died, Robert Estienne left France and went to Geneva, which had become a place of refuge for many scholars, but for over fifty years his descendants carried on a printing establishment in Paris.

Soon it was declared that heresy (saying, writing or teaching anything that was not accepted by the Catholic Church) was to be punishable by death. In 1546 a printer named Dolet was executed and his body burned, together with the books he had published which the Church did not like.

At the time of Dolet's execution there was a young man in Paris who was also to found a great family of printers. His name was Christophe Plantin. He left France and set up his printing establishment in Antwerp. After some ups and downs he became very successful indeed. He was appointed printer to King Philip II of Spain (the Spanish were ruling the Netherlands at that time), and Philip arranged with the Pope that Plantin should print all the service books used in all the countries ruled by Philip. Soon his was the greatest printing office in the world, with twenty-two presses working and a hundred and fifty men employed.

But all the same, everything did not go smoothly with Plantin. His greatest work was a Polyglot Bible printed in four languages—Latin, Greek, Hebrew and Chaldaic. Plantin planned that it was to be in six volumes. It was a tremendous undertaking. King Philip II promised to advance six thousand ducats towards the cost of the work—but we are told that the grants of money did not always arrive. An even greater trouble was that when the book was at last ready (it was printed in the years between 1568 and 1573, and ran into eight volumes instead of six) the King would not allow Plantin to publish it until the Pope gave his permission—and that the Pope refused to do. It was not until there was a new Pope that consent was at last obtained. But even then Plantin's troubles were not over, for one Church authority denounced the book as a work of heresy. The Inquisition, which was a Court set up by the Catholic Church to inquire into and punish heresy, had to see and examine the book before it could be published, and they took years to do it, so that it was only in 1580 that the book could at last be offered for sale.

But by that time fresh troubles had come upon Plantin. The Catholic Spaniards were determined to stamp out heresy in the Netherlands, and the people of the Netherlands, many of whom had become Protestants, were determined to resist. So there was a great deal of fighting, and Antwerp was in the thick of it. In 1576 the city was sacked, and thousands of people were killed, and many houses burnt. Plantin's business, like many others, was almost destroyed. For a time he went to Leyden, where things were calmer, and became printer to the university there. But when things had settled down a little he returned to Antwerp and carried on his business again.

The house in which Plantin lived and ran his business is now a very famous museum which is kept as far as possible just as it was in Plantin's day. It is one of the best places where one can see just what sort of equipment early printers used. Plantin's letters and records have also been preserved and printed so that we know a great deal about him, his business, and the life of his time. We know, for instance, that work started in his printing works at five o'clock in the morning, though there seems to have been no set time for closing.

CHAPTER XVI

*

English Printers and their Difficulties

I n England printers were not interfered with very much for several years after Caxton first introduced printing into the country.

No one tried to stop English printers from printing what they liked or foreign printers and stationers from settling in London, bringing foreign books into the country, and selling them.

But after Luther's preaching had started the Reformation, things began to change. At first King Henry VIII was against Luther—you remember he wrote a book that caused the Pope to give him the title of 'Defender of the Faith'. But before long Henry quarrelled with the Pope, who would not consent to his divorcing his first wife, Catherine of Aragon, and Henry had himself declared head of the Church in England.

For years after that there were disputes and disagreements between those who clung to the old Catholic faith and recognized the Pope as head of the Church everywhere, and those who accepted Henry as head of the Church in England. In time most of the people in England became Protestants.

All through the sixteenth century printers had to be very careful indeed if they were to avoid trouble with one side or the other. During the latter part of Henry VIII's reign and that of his son, Edward VI, printers were not allowed to print or import Catholic books, but during the reign of Mary, who was a Catholic, Protestant books were not allowed. Then Elizabeth, a Protestant, came to the throne, and Catholic literature was once more forbidden.

One result of the Reformation was that people everywhere wanted copies of the Bible in their own languages so that they could read it for themselves. You remember that in England Wyclif had translated the Bible into English in the fourteenth century, long before the days of printing. His translation was, of course, from the Vulgate. After Erasmus's edition of the New Testament in Greek had been published in 1516, William Tyndale began a translation of it into English, but as he did not get much encouragement in England he went away to Hamburg, and later to Cologne, where in 1525 he began to print his English Bible. But the enemies of the Reformation drove him out, and he went to Worms, where a famous printer called Peter Schoeffer printed three thousand copies for him.

Copies of Tyndale's New Testament reached England in 1526, but the Church and the Government in England condemned the book because, being translated from Greek, it was different in some ways from the Latin New Testament they were used to. So Tyndale's New Testament was never really accepted in England, and he himself was executed as a heretic in 1536. Before his death he had revised his New Testament and had translated part of the Old Testament from Hebrew. These translations of Tyndale's were used by a follower of his named Miles Coverdale, who, under the protection of Henry VIII and his minister, Thomas Cromwell, produced the first complete English Bible to be printed in England. It was dedicated to Henry VIII, as head of the English Church. A little later Coverdale revised it and Henry VIII licensed it and, in 1539, gave orders through Thomas

Cromwell that a copy was to be placed in every parish church in England for anyone to read.

Special reading desks were set up to support the big heavy books, and the Bibles were usually attached to the desks by strong chains so that they should not be taken away. In a few places you can still see one of the ancient chained Bibles fastened to its original desk. There is one at Shorwell in the Isle of Wight and others are at Worcester, Lingfield in Surrey, York, Stratford-on-Avon, Backford in Cheshire, and several other places.

A chained Bible

This Bible of Coverdale's was called the Great Bible. Six copies were put in different parts of St. Paul's Cathedral in London, and we are told that crowds gathered round to hear it read, even when Mass was being celebrated.

The printing of copies of the English Bible was stopped when Mary came to the throne, but Englishmen escaped to Geneva and carried on the work there. In 1560 they produced the first small Bible that people could buy for use in their own homes. For the first time, too, the English Bible was printed in Roman type instead of in Gothic, or black letter as it is usually called. And the printers divided the Bible into verses, too, as you remember the French printer, Estienne, had done when he printed his Greek New Testament in Paris in 1551.

In James I's reign it was decided that the English Bible should be revised and an edition printed that should be as correct as it was possible to make it. James I appointed fifty-four scholars from London, Oxford and Cambridge to do the work and it took them four years. The James I Bible, which is called the Authorized Version, appeared in 1611, and it was considered to be absolutely right and final. On the title-page of the Bible is printed:

'Newly translated out of the Originall tongues and with the former translations diligently compared and revised by His Majesties speciall Commandment.'

But, as you read earlier, the men who had prepared the Authorized Version for the press were up against a difficulty, though they did not realize it at the time. The manuscript copies of the New Testament from which Erasmus and all other editors and translators had worked up to that time were very *late* copies. Erasmus and the others had accepted them as being correct, but the books had been copied and re-copied for fourteen hundred years, and all kinds of errors had crept in.

This was made clear when the Codex Alexandrinus which the Patriarch of Constantinople presented to the English king arrived in England in 1627. It was the oldest Bible anyone in western Europe had ever seen, and it showed scholars that there were great differences between one manuscript copy of the Bible and another. It set people hunting for the oldest manuscripts of any parts of the Bible they could find—and the hunt is still going on. Discoveries that have been made from time to time have led to numerous revisions and re-translations as scholars try to get our Bible nearer to the words that were originally written.

From the time when the English Bible was first made available to everyone it had a very great influence on English people, on the way they wrote and talked and on the way they lived and thought. A great many of the people who had copies of the Bible in the sixteenth and seventeenth centuries had no other books at all. They looked upon the Bible as their guide in everything they did. Many of them came to disapprove as much of the way the services were conducted in the Protestant churches that were established in England under Elizabeth as they did of the Catholic services. They believed that bishops and archbishops were unnecessary, and that surplices, crosses, even such symbols as the ring in marriage, were Catholic superstitions which should be abolished. The people who felt like this—the Puritans—increased in numbers until in the middle of the seventeenth century, as you know, there was Civil War, the Puritans won and executed King Charles I, and for a time they ruled England under Oliver Cromwell.

All these things were the result, in some ways, of the printing press, which not only made copies of the Bible available to everyone, but which helped to spread ideas and beliefs in a way that was impossible when every book had to be slowly copied by hand.

Gutenberg when he started printing in Mainz, and Caxton when he set up his first press in Westminster, cannot have had any idea of the tremendous results that were going to follow from the practice of this new art.

But, as you know by now, during the greater part of the sixteenth and seventeenth centuries printers were not free to print what they liked, and the Catholics on the one hand and the Puritans on the other were both persecuted.

In 1407, long before the days of printing, the craftsmen who supplied the scribes with parchment, pens, book-binding materials and so on, formed themselves into a Guild (as most traders and craftsmen did during the Middle Ages) called the

Guild of Stationers. After the introduction of printing the stationers often sold printed books which they had imported from abroad and bound themselves, and sometimes they themselves were also printers.

In 1542 the Guild of Stationers appealed to the Crown for a Charter, which was granted. Under the Charter no one was allowed to practise the 'Art or Mystery of Printing' unless he was a Member of the Company (or Guild) of Stationers, and the Master and Wardens of the Company were given the power to search any house or shop and to seize any forbidden books and imprison the people who printed or sold them.

Stationers were forbidden to import books from abroad, and the law directed that no one who was not an Englishman might carry on business as a stationer at all, and no boy who was not English could be apprenticed to a stationer or printer. This helped to increase the use of English, instead of Latin or French, in English literature, which was not a bad thing, but it also cut English people off from work that was being written and printed in the rest of Europe.

But the most serious restriction that was put upon printers was that they were forbidden to print anything until it had been licensed by officials appointed by the king or queen. This meant that people who wanted to express opinions that were not popular with the Government could only do it if they set up secret presses in garrets and cellars, and printed and distributed their books in secret. They were in constant danger of being caught and severely punished.

Some of the earliest of the Puritans did this successfully for about five years. From 1588 books began to appear that denounced the archbishops and bishops and criticized the way in which the Church conducted its services and the way it neglected the poor and ignorant. The name of the author of the books was given as 'Martin Marprelate'. The name 'Marprelate' is a made up one, meaning 'against the bishops', and no one has ever proved for certain who Martin Marprelate really was. But it seems very likely that he was a Welshman named John Penry who was finally executed for having written something disrespectful about Queen Elizabeth.

'Censorship', as control of written and printed work is called, went on for a long time. John Milton, the great poet who wrote *Paradise Lost* and who was himself a Puritan, living at a time when Puritans were ruling the country, was one of the people who thought printers should be free to print whatever they liked. He wrote a famous pamphlet which he called *Areopagitica; a Speech of Mr. John Milton for the Liberty of Unlicensed Printing*, in which he said something that has often been quoted:

'As good, almost, kill a man as a good book. Who kills a man kills a reasonable creature, God's image; but he who destroys a good book kills reason itself, kills the image of God, as it were, in the eye.'

Milton's protest did not have much effect at the time. Nearly twenty years later, in 1663, a Licensing Act was passed through Parliament. By that Act everything written about politics had to be passed by the Secretary of State before it could be published; everything written about law had to be passed by the Lord Chancellor; most other books had to be passed by the Archbishop of Canterbury and the Bishop of London. Only twenty master-printers were allowed to do business in England, and they were all either in London or at one of the university presses at Oxford and Cambridge.

When William of Orange, in 1688, was invited to come to England by people who were dissatisfied with James II, he landed at Torbay and wanted to have a manifesto printed, but he found that, although two hundred years had passed since Caxton introduced printing into England, there was not a single printer in Exeter or anywhere round about.

CHAPTER XVII

★

More and More Books

Although printers in England worked under difficulties during the sixteenth and seventeenth centuries, nevertheless books of all kinds did pour from the presses, and were eagerly read by the people who could get hold of them—and very queer and interesting books some of them were.

First of all, of course, there were the 'classics'—the books, or all that remained of them, that had been written in Ancient Greece and Rome. Sometimes these were printed in Latin and Greek, and sometimes in English translations. And there was the work of English poets of earlier centuries, such as Langland and Chaucer, and of the historians of the past, such as Higden.

But the real novelties were the work of living authors. There were books on medicine and surgery, some of which would horrify any modern doctor. And there were some very interesting books describing the voyages and adventures of travellers such as Sir Francis Drake, and books giving accounts of strange lands across the sea and the amazing things that were to be seen in them.

During the sixteenth century new schools were being founded, and a few thoughtful people were trying to find new and better ways of educating children. A man named Roger Ascham, who was a great Latin and Greek scholar, and tutor to Queen Elizabeth, wrote a new Latin grammar. It had a very long title of which the first words were *The Schole Master, or plain and perfite way of teaching children to understand, write and speak the Latin tongue.* Perhaps you don't think this sounds very interesting, but it shows that at least one man was trying to make the work of schoolboys a little easier.

Other books were printed for the first time on such subjects as arithmetic, geometry, navigation, anatomy, astronomy and other sciences. They seem quaint to us now and often the authors said things that we now know to be wrong, but they were men who were keenly interested in everything around them and were working and studying and searching for the truth.

Books about religion were published in the sixteenth century, though they were very different from the kind of book that had been written when England was a Catholic country. One that was very popular and that was read almost as much as the Bible itself, was written by a man named John Foxe. It, too, had a very long title, but it was, and still is, usually called Foxe's Book of Martyrs. It described the persecutions by the Catholics of people who wrote and preached and worked for the Reformation.

New history books were being written, too, including one by a man named Raphael Holinshed, who is especially interesting to us because Shakespeare used Holinshed's book in writing his historical plays.

The complete works of Shakespeare himself were not printed until 1623, although he died in 1616, and this 'first folio of Shakespeare', as it is called, is one of the world's most valuable printed books. As much as £23,000 has been paid for a copy. How surprised the printer, who sold the book for one pound when it was first published, would have been if he had known—and Shakespeare, too.

The works of many other great poets, playwrights, scientists and thinkers of the time were preserved for us by the printing press, without which they might have been lost. And some, too, of the popular ballads and romances written by unknown poets of the Middle Ages, and passed on from minstrel to minstrel.

At first the people who set up in business as printers did everything themselves, from cutting or casting their own type to binding and selling the finished book. Many of them, as you have seen, even wrote, or translated, the books they were going to print. If you wanted a book in the early days of printing you went to the place where books were printed, just as, if you wanted a pair of shoes, you went to the man who made them. Printers, too, would take their wares to the great fairs and offer them for sale.

But as time passed and there were more and more books in the world, and more and more people wanting them, it became impossible for the printers to do everything. So some people set up in business as type-founders, and any printer could buy a fount of type from them instead of having to design and make his own. Other people did nothing but bind books after the printers had printed them, and others opened shops in which they sold books not in any way made by themselves.

At first, too, the printers were kept busy printing copies of the many books that already existed in manuscript, but when they began to print the works of authors who were writing quite new books, they had to find the authors and buy their books from them. In time certain people did this work only—they bought the books from the authors and arranged for printers to print them—in other words, they became publishers.

Sometimes all these different businesses—typefounders, printers, bookbinders, publishers, booksellers—were quite separate, but often in the early days two or more would be combined. For a long time, for instance, booksellers were often also publishers.

In the days before printing the people who wrote books, the authors, if they were not monks, were usually attached to the household of some great man. They were servants, just as the scribes and the minstrels were. After printed books became common, the author still had to try to find a patron, some great or wealthy man who would help to support him. The booksellers or publishers did not pay the authors very much for their books. Sometimes the only payment the author got was a certain number of copies of the book he had written, which he could sell himself. He might receive a little money as well.

A writer named John Stow, who wrote a wonderful *Survey of London*, published in 1598, which perhaps you will read one day, received in payment for it the sum of three pounds and forty copies of the book. As Stow had given up his business as a tailor in order to study and write history, it's not surprising that he was very poor in his old age. King James I was told about it, but all that was done for Stow was to grant him permission to collect 'voluntary contributions and kind gratuities' from the king's subjects—which means to beg.

One reason why the bookseller-publishers or printer-publishers could not pay writers very much for their books was because as soon as a book was printed and offered for sale other printers could print copies of it and sell it themselves, and it was very difficult to stop them. Printers who were Members of the Stationers' Company could enter the titles of any books they printed in a register kept by the company, and that gave them the sole right to print the book, and made them (not the authors) the owners of it. In very old books you will sometimes see a note that it has been 'Entered at Stationers' Hall'. That means entered in the register, and is a warning to other printers that they must not copy it.

But as time went on there were more and more printers who were not members of the Stationers' Company, in spite of the laws which, in the seventeenth century, decreed that if any unauthorized person set up a press he was to be 'set in the pillorie and whipt through the City of London'. Printers who were not members of the Company could not enter their books at Stationers' Hall.

Since the seventeenth century various laws, called Copyright Acts, have been made protecting authors and publishers, so that now it is not lawful to print and publish an author's work without permission and payment.

In the eighteenth century a fairly common way for authors to find money on which to live when they were writing, or editing, books, was to open a Subscription List. This meant that they got a large number of people to pay half the price of the book when they added their names to the list, and to promise to pay the other half when the book was finished and delivered. Sometimes this worked very well and sometimes rather badly. Dr. Johnson edited an edition of Shakespeare's plays in this way. But the work took him nine years to do, and by that time all the money he had collected had gone, and, what must have been very worrying indeed, he had lost the list of people who had subscribed!

Gradually publishers became entirely separate from booksellers and printers, and the way in which publishers and authors did business together changed in many ways. For a long time publishers usually paid authors a definite sum of money for a book and then they, the publishers, became the sole owners of the book and could publish it when and how they liked. But another system, called the royalty system, gradually became common. Under this system the book still remained the property of the author, and the publishers paid all the cost of having it printed and published and gave the author so much for each copy they sold.

Nowadays some publishers, for certain kinds of books, still buy the work outright for a settled sum, but the royalty system is more usual.

CHAPTER XVIII

*

Pictures in Books

You remember that when Gutenberg and his followers first began printing, their great aim was to make their printed books as beautiful as the best manuscript books, so that people would hardly know the difference. They even had them illuminated by hand, as the manuscript books had been. But, of course, this could not go on. It made the books too expensive, and printers such as Aldus of Venice and many others saw that books must be printed simply and cheaply so that people who were not very wealthy could afford to buy them.

This, of course, was a very good thing, but unfortunately it meant that some printers no longer bothered to make their books look nice, or cared whether the type was well designed and well arranged on the paper, or even, sometimes, whether the impression was well and clearly printed so that the book was easy to read.

Of course, this wasn't true of all printers. A great many well-designed and well-printed books appeared in Italy, Germany, France and Holland during the fifteenth and sixteenth centuries, and some of them had very interesting and sometimes very beautiful pictures.

You remember that printed pictures really came before printed books. Drawings of religious subjects, such as the St.

Pictures in Books

Christopher you read about in Chapter XII, were made on
blocks of pear or apple or some similar wood, and the background was cut away with a knife, leaving the drawing
raised. Prints of the drawing were taken on sheets of paper.

The first printed pictures that appeared in printed books
were cut on wood blocks in the same way. We call printing
from a raised surface in this way 'letterpress' printing. Quite
early in the history of printing we find that the pictures were
sometimes cut out of metal blocks instead of wooden ones,
but the part that was to be inked was still the raised part, and
the background was cut away.

The first printer to print books with pictures was Albrecht
Pfister of Bamberg, and his first illustrated book appeared in
1461. At first the pictures had to be printed separately and
spaces had to be left for them in the written matter. But before long printers learnt how to print the picture and the type
all at the same time.

The earliest pictures were in simple outline and were intended to be coloured by hand.

But before long the men who cut the pictures on wood became very much cleverer. They were able to show much more
detail, to cut finer lines, and to show light and shade.

One of the best illustrated books of the fifteenth century
was printed at Mainz in 1486. It described the journey of a
man named Bernhard von Breydenback, who went on a pilgrimage to the Holy Land. He took with him an artist named
Reuwich, who made drawings of the places they passed
through and the things they saw. Woodcuts were made from
these drawings to illustrate the book. That makes the book
especially interesting, because in those days if an artist had
to make a picture of a city or place he generally did it from
his imagination, and the picture could not possibly be anything like the real place.

All the same, Breydenback and his companions seem to

have seen some very strange sights on their travels, for there are a great many pictures of animals, including such fabulous beasts as salamanders and unicorns!

A very interesting illustrated book published at Nuremberg in 1493 is usually called the *Nuremberg Chronicle*. It was a tremendous job, as six hundred and forty-five separate woodcut blocks were used. They represented portraits of great and famous men, saints, scenes from history and from the Bible, views of cities, and all kinds of other things. But the pictures were not all different. The same portraits appeared again and again—only the name of the man or woman they were supposed to represent being changed. The same view of a city did duty for a whole number of different cities. The same picture of a saint represented a variety of saints in different parts of the book.

This seems funny to us now, but it was not at all uncommon in those days. A printer would use the same block many times in the same book, or in several different books.

One of the first books with humorous pictures was printed in Basle in 1497. It was called the *Navis Stultifera*, which means the Ship of Fools. On every page there was a picture of a man dressed as a clown, or wearing a fool's cap and bells, and doing something that the artist thought ridiculous. For instance, there is one picture of a man who is called a 'Bibliomaniac', which means a man who is mad about books. He is sitting in a big carved chair before a desk, with books lying or standing on shelves all round him. He is wearing huge spectacles, and the hood that hangs behind his neck is decorated with bells, and has two points hanging from it with bells on the ends, like a fool's cap. He has a kind of dusting brush in his hand, and he is saying: 'I have the first place among fools, for I have heaps of books which I rarely open. If I read them I forget them and am no wiser.'

In many of these early books we are told who was the

author and who was the printer, but we are very seldom told the name of the artist who made the drawings, or of the engraver who cut them on the wood or metal block. Sometimes the artist and the engraver were the same man, but more often they were not.

In Italy and France Missals and Books of Hours and similar Church books were printed, and the drawings in them were sometimes coloured by hand in order to imitate as exactly as possible the illuminated manuscripts. But before the end of the sixteenth century, in Italy, printers began to experiment in quite a new way of making coloured pictures. They printed several blocks, one on top of another, each block being printed in a different colour. It was the very beginning of a method of colour printing that is still used to-day, and that you will be reading more about later.

A book that was very popular in the fifteenth and sixteenth centuries was called *The Dance of Death*. The first edition of it was printed in France in 1485. It had seventeen pictures showing Death visiting all kinds of people from Popes and Kings down to poor peasants. It was not a very cheerful subject, but people seem to have liked it, and pictures of the same kind were often painted on the walls of buildings. The most famous of *The Dance of Death* books was one printed in Germany in 1538, in which the illustrations were the work of the great artist Hans Holbein who spent a good deal of his life in England and painted portraits of Henry VIII and many of the people of his Court. Holbein did fifty-eight drawings altogether for *The Dance of Death*, and most of them are believed to have been cut on the wood blocks by a very famous engraver called Hans Hutzelburger. Many people think that these Dance of Death pictures of Holbein's are the very finest sixteenth-century woodcuts there are.

Holbein did a great many illustrations for other books, including the New Testament.

Another great German artist who designed a large number of illustrations for books was Albrecht Dürer. A very famous work of his was a series of pictures illustrating the Apocalypse —which, you remember, was the name given to the last book in the Bible, the Book of Revelation. They were very strong, vigorous pictures, and you quite often see some of them reproduced to-day, especially perhaps one called 'The Four Horsemen'.

Pictures printed in English books in the fifteenth and sixteenth centuries were a long way behind those in the books you have just been reading about. There seem to have been no good artists or engravers in England in Caxton's time, or for a long time after, and the pictures he and most of his followers printed were very simple outline drawings. They are quaint and amusing but not very beautiful.

Later on, in the last half of the sixteenth century, several English books appeared with much better pictures. Many of them were published by a famous printer named John Daye. Foxe's *Book of Martyrs* and Holinshed's *Chronicle* both had good pictures, but no one knows whether they were the work of English artists and engravers or not.

You read on page 157 that printing from a raised surface is called letterpress printing. There is another way of printing which is called 'intaglio'.

In intaglio printing the drawing is made on a copper plate and the lines that are going to print are cut into the plate with a sharp tool. In letterpress printing, you remember, it is the background that is cut away.

When the intaglio plate is inked, the ink fills the sunken lines. Then the surface of the plate—the part that is not to print—is wiped quite clean. A damp sheet of paper is put over the plate, and the paper and the plate are pressed between heavy rollers. The ink is pulled out of the sunken lines on to the paper.

'The Four Horsemen' by Dürer

Copperplate engravings, as such pictures are called, were known before printing with movable type was invented, just as block prints were. But the first printers who put printed pictures into their books used wood blocks, and although some of them tried using copperplate engravings quite early, they were not very successful and soon gave up. One reason was that the engravings could not be printed at the same time as the type. They had to be printed separately either into spaces left for them on the printed sheet, which was difficult, or else on separate sheets of paper which could afterwards be pasted into the book. You can see that all this made far more work and made the books more expensive.

So for a time books were illustrated almost entirely with pictures cut in relief on wood or metal blocks, except when the picture had to be very accurate and detailed, such as the diagrams in scientific books. But as time went on engravings became more and more popular, until at last, in books which well-to-do people could afford to pay for, they took the place of woodcuts altogether, and woodcuts were only used in cheaper books.

CHAPTER XIX

★

Englishmen who tried to make Printed Books
more Beautiful

Unfortunately very few of the books that were printed in England during the sixteenth and seventeenth centuries were beautiful in themselves.

Perhaps one reason was that English printers were often printing work that had not been licensed, and so were in a great hurry to get the work done and away before inspectors came to visit their establishments and cause trouble. Often, too, even a small piece of printing would be divided between two or three printers, because if any trouble followed it was more difficult for the authorities to trace where the book had been produced than if all the work had been done by one printer. Also, no English printer had many presses or founts of type in those days, so the work of printing a full-sized book might be divided between as many as four firms—and beautiful books cannot be produced in that way.

Until the eighteenth century most English printers bought their types and their best papers from Holland. The Dutch were famous for their typefounding. Then, in 1720, an Englishman named William Caslon designed and cast a fount of type which did a great deal to improve English printing.

It was the most beautiful series of type characters that had been made in England up to that time. It is still used by printers.

But a man named John Baskerville, who was living at the same time as Caslon, is even more important in the history of English printing. He was not a printer in his early days. He started out in life as servant to a clergyman in Birmingham, but he could write so beautifully that he soon became writing-master at a local school. Then, because he wanted to make more money, he took to manufacturing articles that were very popular indeed in his day—glossy, lacquered trays and little boxes, and that kind of thing, called japanned goods. He was very successful and made a big fortune. Then, when he was fifty years old, he took up printing as a hobby. He made up his mind to print only a few books, but to print them just as perfectly as it was possible for him to do it.

He started by designing and making his type. Then he had his press made—the same kind of press as other printers were using, but made more carefully and exactly. He did not like the paper that was being used at the time. The screen through which the pulp was drained in making paper had long wires which made lines on the finished paper. So he thought out a new way of making the screen so that there was a closely woven web of wires which did not mark the paper. He had paper made to his order, which is called 'wove' paper to distinguish it from the other kind, which is called 'laid' paper.

He made his own printing inks, too, because the ink of the time was not good enough for his purpose. In fact, there was no single detail of printing that he did not attend to and think out for himself, so that it could be done as perfectly as possible, and he introduced ways of doing some things that had never been tried before. For instance, as his sheets were printed they were put between hot plates of copper. That

164

D. JUNII

JUVENALIS

ET

AULI

PERSII FLACCI

SATYRAE.

BIRMINGHAMIAE:

Typis JOHANNIS BASKERVILLE.

M DCC LXI.

A title-page by Baskerville

set the ink and gave the paper a polished look that no other printers had ever produced.

Baskerville took seven years to get his printing establishment ready. Then, at last, after several postponements, his first book was issued. It was a copy of Virgil, and immediately made Baskerville famous as a printer.

The reason why Baskerville's books were so much better than any others being produced at the time was because he had designed a series of beautiful letters, and he arranged them carefully on the page, taking great care to see that they were properly spaced and in the right positions.

Baskerville's letters led the way to a kind of type which we call 'modern'. The kind of roman letter that had been used before, and which Caslon designed, is called 'old-style'. These two kinds of type are still used and it is not very easy for people who are not printers to tell the difference between them. The chief difference is that in 'modern' type there is more contrast between the thick and thin strokes in each letter than in old style. The serifs in modern type are thin and sharp pointed at the ends, while those in old-style are rounded at the ends.

Altogether Baskerville printed about sixty-seven books, including an edition of the Bible. His books were rather expensive, because he gave so much time and thought to preparing them, so they could only be bought by well-to-do people. In a preface to Milton's *Paradise Lost*, he wrote:

'It is not my desire to print many books: but such only as are books of consequence, of intrinsic merit, or established reputation, and which the public may be pleased to see in an elegant dress and to purchase at such a price as will repay the extraordinary care and expense that must necessarily be bestowed upon them.'

Baskerville's work had a tremendous influence on other printers in other parts of Europe, who imitated his 'modern' type and 'wove' paper, and his way of arranging the type on the page. So for a little while England was a leader and set the fashion for other countries.

Another 'amateur' printer of the eighteenth century was Horace Walpole, who, towards the end of his life, became fourth Earl of Oxford. He set up a printing press in an extraordinary house, rather like a Gothic castle, that he built for himself near Twickenham. It was called Strawberry Hill. The first book printed at the Strawberry Hill Press was a book of poems by the poet Thomas Gray, who was a great friend of Walpole's. Many of Walpole's own books were first printed at his own press. His work, like Baskerville's, helped to teach people what a really well-printed book looked like, and to notice the difference between good and bad type, and good and bad arrangement.

It was during the eighteenth century that the finest copperplate engravings for book illustrations were made. Clever artists did the pictures, which were then passed on to the engravers who carefully copied them upon the copper plate.

Some of the best work during the eighteenth century was done in France. It was very dainty and graceful, like the French pictures that were being painted at the time, and which you can see in such places as Hertford House in London where the Wallace Collection is kept. In the paintings, and in the illustrations and decorations in the books, there are nymphs and cupids, wreaths and flowers, picturesque ruins, and other graceful, pretty and not very serious things.

This kind of art and book illustration came to an end with the French Revolution.

But by that time very fine work was being done in England. Early in the century the first really great original English artist, Hogarth, designed and engraved pictures for books, but later he drew and engraved whole sets of pictures that told a story without any words—but they are not really part of the story of the book. Towards the end of the century a very great genius indeed appeared—William Blake.

Blake's engravings were quite different from anything that had been done by any other artist. He had a wonderful imagination and his pictures, which he both drew and engraved himself, were weird and mysterious and strange. You can see some of his pictures in the Victoria and Albert Museum in London. He illustrated the poetry of Milton and Dante, and did a famous series of illustrations for the Book of Job.

Blake was a poet as well as an artist. I expect you know his poems 'Little Lamb who made Thee?' and 'Tiger, tiger, burning bright'. They come from two books of poems, *Songs of Innocence* and *Songs of Experience*, which Blake wrote and illustrated. He engraved the words as well as the pictures in his books. Sometimes the pictures were printed in colours and sometimes tinted by hand.

By this time, the second half of the eighteenth century, people had been keen on copperplate engravings for so long that the people who made woodcuts had not had a chance. So woodcuts had become very bad indeed. Then, in 1753, a boy was born who when he grew up was to become a very famous artist and who was to help to make woodcuts, or rather wood-engravings, fashionable and popular again. His name was Thomas Bewick.

The earlier woodcuts had been cut on blocks of pear or apple wood, cut from the length of the tree—that is, the way of the grain—and the tool used was a small knife which was held rather like a pen and drawn towards the worker. Bewick worked quite differently. He worked on the wood of the box tree, which is very hard, and he had blocks cut across the grain of the wood. He used the same pointed tools, called gravers, that the engravers on metal used. The worker used the tool by pushing it away from him.

These differences are very important because they made it possible for Bewick to make wood-engravings such as had never been seen before.

Bewick illustrated a book of *Select Fables* which was a great success, so he was encouraged to start work on something he had wanted to do for some time. That was to make a whole series of engravings to illustrate a *General History of Quadrupeds*. It was a very big job, and it took Bewick six years, working mostly in the evenings. One of his difficulties was to find examples of all the animals he wanted to make pictures of, so you can guess how pleased he was when a travelling menagerie came to Newcastle, which was the town nearest to his home at Ovingham in Northumberland.

The book on quadrupeds appeared in 1790 and sold so well that it had to be reprinted in 1791 and again in 1792. People liked it, not only because the drawings of animals were the best that had appeared up to that time, but because Bewick had drawn charming little scenes from country life as tail-pieces—which is what the little drawings that sometimes appear at the end of chapters are called. One of these shows a baby in a field pulling a pony's tail, while its mother comes running to save it from being kicked or trampled on.

After his book on quadrupeds Bewick started on another book that is even more famous, a *History of British Birds*. Here he didn't have to worry about models, for he knew and loved every bird that flew. He did two books, one on land birds and one on water birds, and they were both received with delight.

There has always been something about printing that has appealed to 'amateurs' like Baskerville and Walpole—people who did not have to earn their living by printing but who loved beautiful books. Another very famous amateur printer was William Morris. He was born in 1834 and he became tremendously interested in the crafts that used to be done by hand in the Middle Ages, but which are done by machinery now. ◢

Morris hated mass-production, and felt that the machine had destroyed the beauty and character that there used to be in hand-woven materials, tapestry, stained-glass windows and all kinds of other things—including, of course, books.

Morris practised various handicrafts himself, and he and the artists he was associated with, such as Rossetti and Burne-Jones, designed beautiful things and tried to improve people's taste, so that they would not put up with ugly things. Then Morris decided to become a printer, and he started a private printing office called the Kelmscott Press. He designed a type something like the Roman one Jenson designed at Venice in 1476 and called it the 'Golden' type, and he designed a Gothic type which he called 'Troy' type. His presses were hand-presses, such as the early printers had used, and he used hand-made paper. He designed initial letters, borders and ornaments, and tried to make his books as beautiful and individual as the manuscript books and the first printed books had been.

Morris issued fifty books during the seven years his press was working. His masterpiece was an edition of the works of Chaucer, which was illustrated by Burne-Jones. His printers were working on it for five years, and the first two bound copies were handed to him in June 1896, only four months before he died.

Neither Morris nor anyone else can stop people from using machinery and make them go back to doing everything by hand. But he and people like him do help to remind us that the things we use can be well designed and beautiful, or badly designed and ugly. As regards books, there would be very few and they would all be very expensive if they were all printed on hand-presses as Morris would have liked.

Although some printers and publishers of the present day

do turn out bad books, most of them go to a great deal of trouble to see that their books are well designed and well printed. And most of them realize how very important their work is.

In some printers' offices you can see the following words printed, framed and hung up in the entrance, and if you were to visit the Government Printing Office in Washington you would find them on a bronze plaque:

THIS IS A
PRINTING-OFFICE
CROSS-ROADS OF CIVILISATION
REFUGE OF ALL THE ARTS AGAINST THE RAVAGES OF TIME
ARMOURY OF FEARLESS TRUTH AGAINST WHISPERING RUMOUR
INCESSANT TRUMPET OF TRADE
FROM THIS PLACE WORDS MAY FLY ABROAD
NOT TO PERISH AS WAVES OF SOUND BUT FIXED IN TIME
NOT CORRUPTED BY THE HURRYING HAND BUT VERIFIED IN
PROOF
FRIEND, YOU STAND ON SACRED GROUND:
THIS IS A PRINTING-OFFICE.

CHAPTER XX

*

Books for Children

If, somehow, you could take yourself back to a shop in which books were sold during the first two or three hundred years of printing, you would find it different in many ways from a bookshop of to-day. For one thing, the books would not have gay, brightly coloured paper wrappers, as many have now. Those which were already bound would usually be dark in colour, with leather covers, and would be solid and very strong looking. But a great many of the books would not be bound at all, as people often bought books just as they came from the printers and had them bound themselves.

But there is something else very important that I am sure you would notice. You would find no books written especially for children. Nowadays every bookshop has at least a few shelves on which there are nothing but children's books, and many of the bigger shops have a large children's department with assistants who do nothing else but look after it. It would have been no use a bookseller of the sixteenth century devoting even one shelf to children's books, for he would have had nothing to put on it.

Of course, school books such as Roger Ascham's Latin Grammar were printed, and books on how to behave, but I don't think you would have found them very attractive. For one thing, they had no pictures. The first book with pictures ever to be used in schools did not appear until 1658. It was called *The Visible World,* and contained a number of little woodcuts with descriptions of them in Latin and English. About the same time books with pictures of objects whose names began with the different letters of the alphabet began

A horn book

to appear, which were intended to help little children to learn their ABC. But they were nothing like the large gaily coloured picture books that people buy for tiny children to-day. The pictures were only about an inch square and they were not very well printed.

For about two hundred years before that, and for about a hundred and fifty years after, children usually learned the alphabet from something which was called a horn-book—

though you probably would not consider that it was a book at all. It was made from a thin oak board, shaped like a little oblong bat with a short handle. A piece of paper on which the alphabet was printed was placed on the board, and a sheet of thin transparent horn was put over it to protect it, and was held in place by having a narrow strip of brass put round the edge and fastened down with small tacks.

A horn-book which was found in the wall of an old house when it was being destroyed had the back covered with leather, on which a portrait of Charles I on horseback was stamped.

Horn-books seem to have been used only by English-speaking people in England and in America. The first thing on the sheet of paper was generally a cross. Then came the alphabet, first in capitals and then in small letters. Sometimes you read in old books of children learning 'the criss-cross row'. It means learning the ABC—the row of letters following the cross on a horn-book.

After the alphabet came the vowels, and examples of them combined with a consonant. Then came the Lord's Prayer, and, usually, the numerals.

Millions of children must have had their first lessons in reading from a horn-book, the teacher pointing to each letter in turn with a pointer called a fescue. It is to be feared that many horn-books served other purposes, too, for one of their nicknames was 'battledore book', which seems to suggest that on the way home from school they were sometimes used as bats.

The handle of the horn-book usually had a hole in it through which a string was passed so that the horn-book could be attached to the child's girdle, or hung on his wrist.

If children wanted to read story-books during the fifteenth, sixteenth and seventeenth centuries (and I'm quite sure they did) then they had to read the books printed for grown-ups.

There were all the romances which had come down from the Middle Ages—the stories about King Arthur, Sir Bevis of Southampton, Guy of Warwick, and similar people, and the extraordinary adventures they had, and the dragons and giants they slew. Some of these characters have survived in modern children's books, but they were originally meant for grown-up people.

Another book that was very popular in the early days of printing was *Æsop's Fables*. That was not originally a children's book either, but it was used during the sixteenth and seventeenth centuries in school, usually printed in Latin and English. So a great many children must have read it. In the British Museum there is a copy of *Æsopz Fablz*, as the translator calls it, which was published in 1585. But books had a long life in those days, and four different people have signed their names in this particular book. One of them was a little boy who could not write very well, and he possessed the book over a hundred years after it was printed. He wrote in it:

'James Dodson is my name and with my pen i write the same and write the same and if my pen had beene a litle beter I would —— every Letter 1690.'

The word left out is quite unreadable.

But for some thirty years before little James Dodson owned a copy of *Æsop's Fables*, certain people had been writing books especially for children—though not by any means the kind of book you are used to. These people were the Puritans. They were very stern, serious, religious people, and they believed that unless men and women and children led very good lives, terrible things would happen to them after they were dead. So they felt that it was very important indeed to teach children to be good, and they believed that gay, amusing things, such as jokes and games, were wicked. So their books were full of stories about children who died very young, and about the prayers they said, and about their repentance for such sins as sharpening a knife on a Sunday or not reproving someone they had heard swearing.

Such books were meant to make children think about religion and sin. In one of them, by a man named James Janeway, the author asks, towards the end, 'How art thou now affected, poor Child, in the reading of this Book? Have you shed ever a tear since you begun reading?'

Such gloomy books must have caused many children to shed tears. But the writers did not really mean to be unkind. They thought that by making children believe that they were very sinful they were doing the very best they could to help them.

If you had been alive in the eighteenth century you would probably have read books of a very different kind, if you were able to get hold of them. They were called chap-books, because they were carried about the country by pedlars, or chapmen, as such people were called. In those days when there were very few shops in country districts and no buses or trains to take people to the towns, the chapmen were very welcome visitors. In their huge packs they carried all kinds of things—ribbons, laces, medicines, trinkets, and a great many books. The books were very cheap—one penny to sixpence—and were generally quite small, about four inches by two. They were usually very clumsily and badly printed, and the wood blocks that illustrated them were rough and often did not illustrate the story properly. The same picture would appear again and again in different books. Chap-books had paper covers, or no covers at all. The stories were often badly written, in poor English. But, in spite of all this, the chap-books did give country people all over the British Isles something to read, and they kept alive all sorts of stories, songs and fairy tales that might otherwise have been forgotten.

It was not until 1744—only just over two hundred years

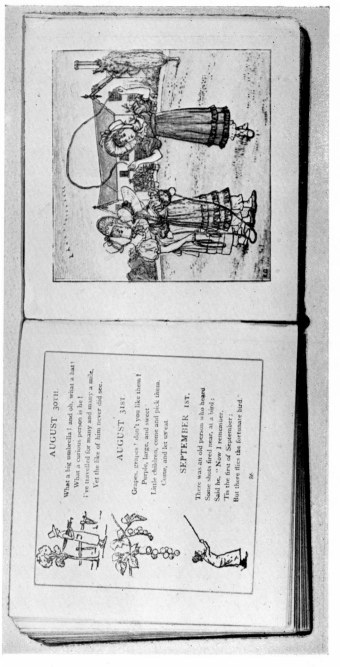

A page from a book by Kate Greenaway

ago—that anyone realized that it was worth while to write and print better books for children to read, and to write them especially so that they would really amuse and please children as well as teaching them something or helping them to be good. The man who first did this was John Newbery, and the first children's book he published was called *A Little Pretty Pocket Book*. He said that it was intended 'for the instruction and amusement of little Master Tommy and pretty

An eighteenth-century pedlar

Miss Polly'. The book cost sixpence, but a ball or a pin-cushion could be bought with it, and the cost was then eight-pence.

The little *Pocket Book* is full of pictures of children playing games. Many of the games are the same as those boys and girls still play—kite-flying, marbles, hide-and-seek, blind-man's-buff, hopscotch, king of the castle, and so on. But cricket looks a little odd, as it is being played with two stumps and a curved bat. Other games are not quite so familiar to most children now perhaps as they were—maypole dancing, for instance, and battledore and shuttlecock. But the interesting thing about Newbery's book is that games and toys are not regarded as something wicked, as they were fifty or sixty years before by the Puritans. And another important thing is that Newbery took a lot of trouble to make his little books look attractive by having them covered in gaily patterned paper and by having special blocks made for them, instead of using any old blocks that happened to be about, whether they were suitable or not.

Although Newbery's book, for the first time, was intended to please and amuse children, it was also meant to instruct them and improve them, if possible. The heading printed above each game is 'The Great A Play', 'The Great B Play', 'The Little a Game', and so on, intended to help children to learn the alphabet, and there are little verses, too, bringing in the letters. Here is one of them:

> *Here's great K and L*
> *Pray Dame can you tell*
> *Who put the Pig-Hog*
> *Down into the well?*

Part of the book is a 'Letter from Jack the Giant Killer'. The ball and pin-cushion bought with the book each had one side red and one black, and Jack tells the children that every time they do a good deed they must stick a pin in the red side and every time they do a bad deed they must stick one in the black side.

Newbery published many other attractive books for children, and other publishers followed his example. During the second half of the eighteenth century quite a large number of people took to writing books especially for children. But for a long time such books were *never* written simply to amuse. They always had to teach something as well, and every story had to have a moral, and to show that such qualities as greed, selfishness, cruelty and quarrelsomeness led to disaster, while their opposites led to happiness.

Some of these books were well written and the characters in them were alive and the stories interesting, so that the names of the writers have lived and their books have not been forgotten. Maria Edgeworth was one of the authors who could write a good story in good English. A book called *Sandford and Merton* by Thomas Day was very popular, and another called *The Fairchild Family* by Mrs. Sherwood. Such books are still sometimes read even to-day. But some of the other books of the time were very solemn and dull.

The dull books were often made interesting by delightful woodcuts by such artists as Thomas Bewick, whom you read about in the last chapter, his brother John, and many other artists. The pictures often showed children natural scenes from country life, animals, birds' nests, shepherds, farmyard scenes and so on, which did more than simply illustrate the rather serious stories.

But there was one kind of story without a moral that appeared in books for children for the first time during the eighteenth century, and that was the fairy tale. Some of the fairy tales were translated from the French—for such stories were very popular among grown-up people in France at that time—and some were the old English tales that had been handed down from one generation to another for hundreds of years. But towards the end of the century many people believed that fairy stories were very bad for children. One lady wrote that the story of Cinderella 'paints some of the worst passions that can enter into the human breast, and of which little children should, if possible, be totally ignorant; such as envy, jealousy, a dislike of mothers-in law (step-mothers) and half-sisters, vanity, a love of dress, etc.' The story of Jack the Giant-Killer was said to be full of 'abominable absurdities', and even Robinson Crusoe was to be kept out of the nursery because his story might lead to 'an early taste for a rambling life and a desire of adventures'—which was evidently not considered a good thing.

So poor Cinderella, Jack, and all their companions were completely banished from a great many nurseries. One publisher, whose name was John Marshall, wrote that the books he published were 'entirely divested of the prejudicial Nonsense (to young Minds) the Tales of Hobgoblins, Witches, Fairies, Love, Gallantry, etc. . . .'

But somehow, in spite of it all, the fairy tale characters survived.

Of course, there were people who did not agree with those who disapproved of fairy tales and nursery rhymes. The writer Charles Lamb was furious with them, and called them 'those blights and blasts of all that is human in man and child'.

At the beginning of the nineteenth century books with a moral continued to be written, but for the first time a few books of a different kind also appeared. One of the earliest was called *The Butterfly's Ball and Grasshopper's Feast*, and was by a Mr. William Roscoe. *The Butterfly's Ball* did not try to teach anybody anything, neither had it any moral. It was just a lively poem telling of the revels of the butterfly and the grasshopper and their friends, and it was illustrated with jolly pictures of children and insects. It was a great success at once and a large number of imitations appeared during the next few years.

Such books as these were sometimes sold 'plain'—that is, with the pictures simply printed in black and white—and sometimes 'coloured'. When they were coloured the tints were put on by a number of girls of about thirteen or fourteen years old who sat round a table, each one with a paint-brush and a pan of paint. The sheets on which the pictures had been printed were passed round. The first girl painted one colour, perhaps red, in the right places, according to a finished copy that was set before them. Then she passed the picture on to the next girl, who painted in the blue, or yellow, or whatever might be necessary, and so on all round the table. Meanwhile the first girl painted the red on another picture, and then another, and so on until all the pictures for the book were ready.

During the nineteenth century books of all kinds appeared for children. Some of them were interesting and amusing and beautifully illustrated and printed. There were books on how to play various games, and books of pictures of people doing everyday jobs, such as carrying rushes through the streets and calling, 'Any Chairs to mend'. These are very interesting to us to-day because they tell us something about the way people lived and dressed a century or more ago. Sometimes, too, they show us bits of London and other places that have now disappeared. There were books, too, of comic verses and riddles, with funny pictures.

But by far the greater number of children's books were still meant to teach them something, or, even more often, to give them awful warnings about what might happen if they were not awfully good. A little boy who loses his temper is shown growing up to commit a dreadful crime, for which he is executed. A little girl who will not learn to sew is shown gradually becoming more and more ragged until she has no clothes at all and cannot go out.

Some of the books went even further and seemed to want to warn children against doing anything at all. There are pictures of children falling off see-saws, or out of swings, drowning in ponds, going through the ice when skating, being thrown off ponies when riding, tipping off ladders and out of windows—in fact, some of the books contained nothing at all but pictures of disasters, and the reasons for them—which were usually disobedience. One book was actually called *A Chapter of Accidents*, and shows a woman and her basket of apples being tipped out of a cart, from which the wheel has come off; a man being killed by a lion that has somehow got into his room; a stage-coach going over the edge of a quarry —and many other gloomy happenings of the same kind.

Even when children were encouraged by their books to take part in sports and games, they were generally warned not to overdo it, or to allow themselves to become too enthusiastic! Here is the first paragraph on Cricket from a book called *The Instruction and Guide for Little Masters* which was sold for 1s. plain, 2s. coloured. Cricket, we are told, is:

'A Manly exercise! But full of admonition. It is only fit for athletic or strong constitutions. It requires great labour, a constant quick motion of the body; and causes a profusion of sweat in proportion. The secret pleasure in this exercise is to prove yourself a better man than your antagonist but take care you do not overplay your part, and instead of excelling work your ruin and destruction. What will it avail in such a contest to say I have conquered Will or Tom with the loss of my life or with a broken constitution.'

There is a great deal more of the same kind.

Sometimes such books were in the form of dialogues in which one child tells others how the games are to be played. One, called *Juvenile Games for the Four Seasons*, and published in Edinburgh, starts off by explaining that the pictures are different from the descriptions given of them in the dialogues. 'In the Dialogues,' the publisher explains, 'Young Persons of both sexes are introduced in the Games, to render the Work interesting to young ladies as well as gentlemen; but in the plates, they are played at exclusively by young gentlemen, and the reason of this is, that most of the Games require strength and dexterity.'

As some of the games are cup and ball, marbles and draughts, this explanation does not seem very convincing. Probably the publisher had these particular plates by him and did not want to go to the trouble and expense of having others made.

Nevertheless, as the nineteenth century went on, a great many publishers went to a lot of trouble to produce good books for children and to have them well illustrated by good artists. Famous painters of the time were not ashamed to illustrate children's books; neither were the fine artists who illustrated the grown-up books of the nineteenth century— such as George Cruikshank, whose name I expect you have heard, and many others. Cruikshank illustrated the first English translation of Grimm's Fairy Tales, published in 1826.

In 1869 there appeared a famous book which I am sure you have read—*Alice's Adventures in Wonderland* by Lewis Carroll. And though you may have read it in a modern edition I am pretty certain that you picture Alice in your mind almost exactly as she was shown by the artist, John Tenniel, to the children who first read about her. Tenniel and Carroll worked together very closely over the illustrating of the book, and Tenniel's drawings of Alice and of the queer creatures she met seem to fit the story exactly.

There is one thing I am sure you will remember about 'Alice in Wonderland', if you have read it, and that is that it doesn't attempt to teach anything, and there is no moral. It is just an amusing story of a little girl's strange adventures. As the century went on more and more books of this kind were printed, and often they were illustrated by artists who devoted the whole of their time to children's books. One of the most famous of these artists was Kate Greenaway. I expect you know what her little girls looked like, with their long frocks, big sun-bonnets and mittens. Children were not really dressed that way in the 1880's, when she was working, but her books were so popular that she set a fashion, and some people began to dress their children like hers. At weddings and fancy dress dances you still sometimes see children dressed in 'Kate Greenaway' style.

Gradually the 'awful warning' books died out and books for children became more varied until, at the present time, you can go into the children's section of a bookshop and find a book especially written for you on almost any subject you can think of, as well as stories of every kind and description.

CHAPTER XXI

★

How Printing is Done To-day

For about three hundred and fifty years after the invention of printing with movable types printing was done in very much the same way as Gutenberg and Caxton and the other early printers had done it. During the eighteenth century the press itself was often made of iron instead of wood, and there were a few alterations and improvements, but every stage in the printing of a book still had to be done by hand.

The first really big change in England happened in 1814, when for the first time a printing press was made to work by steam power. It was a newspaper that had this first steam-driven press installed, *The Times*, in London. With their new press they could print 1,500 copies of the paper in an hour, which seemed an enormous number in those days. But the actual arranging of the type ready for printing still had to be done by hand.

The arranging of the type, or 'composing' as it is called, is still done by hand for certain kinds of printing, such as handbills, printed cards, headed notepaper, leaflets, etc. A man who is called a compositor stands in front of the 'case', which is the cabinet in which the type-letters are kept, and picks up each letter separately from its special compartment. The case is in two parts. The upper part contains a set of large capital letters, another set of smaller capital letters, and a number of signs and figures that are not as a rule used very often.

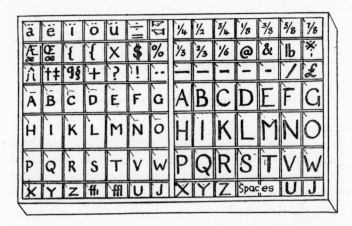

Cases, showing arrangement of the letters

The lower case contains all the small letters, the numerals and a number of other signs. Each letter or sign has its own compartment. In the upper case the compartments are all of the same size, and the letters are arranged alphabetically, except that U and J are put at the end, after Z. That is because when printing first started U and J were not used at all, and by the time they had become general, so that printers had to add them to their founts of type, it was thought simpler to put them at the end of the alphabet rather than insert them in the proper places, and so throw some of the other letters in the case out of position.

In a copy of *A Midsummer Night's Dream* printed as late as 1600, the word 'servants' on the title-page is printed 'seruants'. On the same title-page the W in the name William is made up of two capital V's printed close together, so the printer evidently had not any capital W's in his fount. J did not take the place of I until even later, and in old books you often see names such as Johann spelt Iohann.

In the lower case the compartments are of many different sizes and the letters are not arranged in alphabetical order. That is because some letters are used far more often than others, so that many more of them are required, and they must have bigger compartments. In English the letter e is used more than any other, so its compartment is the largest and is in the most convenient position for the compositor to get at it. On the other hand x is not used very often, so it is tucked away in one corner, and has quite a small compartment.

All the letters and signs in any one case will belong to the same 'fount' of type. That means that they will all be of the same design, or style, and the same size. The different designs each have their own particular name, such as 'Caslon', 'Bodoni', 'Times Roman', and each design is made in a variety of sizes from very small to very large. For a long time the sizes had names, too, such as minikin (which was very small), gem, pearl, minion, long primer, and many others, up to 2-line pica, which was the largest. But this was not very satisfactory, as the sizes were not standardized, and would vary slightly according to the foundry they came from. Early this century English typefounders and printers adopted from America a way of measuring type which is called the 'point' system. A point is just about a seventy-second of an inch, and type-letters are said to be 6-point, 8-point, 10-point, or whatever it may be in depth. The size of the type in which this book is set, for instance, is 11-point, 2-point leaded, which means there is a strip of metal 2-points wide between each line of type.

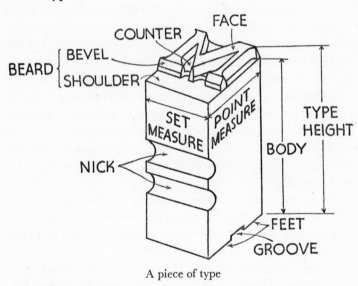

A piece of type

The old names for the type sizes are not used now, except nonpareil, which is 6-point, and pica, which is 12-point.

Each piece of type the compositor takes out of the case consists of a little rectangular column of metal with a letter, or sign, moulded on the top. Every piece of type must be exactly the same height from the base to the surface, or face, of the letter, as every other piece of type. This type-height, as it is called, is ·918 inches. Each section of a piece of type has a name. The drawing will show you what the sections are and what they are called.

The size in points of a type is measured from the front, or belly, of the column, or body, of the type to the back. So if a fount of type is said to be 72-point, or one inch in size (which would be very large indeed, of course), you will not find that the printed letters a, c, x and so on measure one inch, but that the distance from the top of the highest ascender, say in d or l, to the bottom of the lowest descender, say in p or y, is approximately one inch.

You will notice in the drawing that there is a furrow, or nick, on the body of the type. This is very important because it is always on the same side as the base of the letter, and the compositor feels it with his fingers and that helps him to be sure of putting the letter the right way up. Also the nicks are differently arranged for different founts of type.

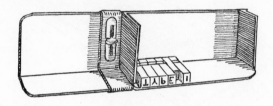

A composing stick

In his hand the compositor holds an instrument called a composing stick. The drawing will show you what that is like. He adjusts it so that it is exactly the right length for the lines he has to make. In it he arranges the letters as he takes them out of the case, and at the end of every word he puts a piece of type with no letter on the top—a space. To make the letters fit exactly into the stick he has to vary the size of the spaces before the line is completed, using wider or narrower ones as required. If the printed lines are to be some distance apart, he must put a strip of metal, called a lead, after each line of type.

When the stick is full the compositor lifts the type out and puts it into a long shallow tray called a galley. Then he fills the stick again and adds that to the galley, and so on until the galley is full. Then the type in the galley is made firm by having strips of wood or metal, which are called furniture, wedged tightly round the edges. The type in the galley is inked by having an inky roller run over it, the galley is put into a small press, with a long strip of paper over it, and an impression is taken which is called a galley-proof. The galley-proof is read and any necessary corrections are made. Then the type is ready to be divided up into pages.

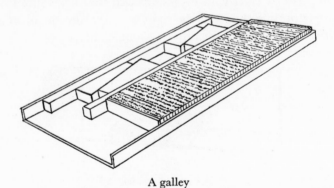

A galley

But nowadays, if the work to be printed is a long one, such as a book, it is not composed by hand in the way I have just described. In 1890 a wonderful machine was invented called a Linotype. The man who works the Linotype sits in front of a little keyboard, something like the keyboard of a typewriter. As he taps each key on the keyboard a mould, called a matrix, for the appropriate letter is carried along a belt and put into a box, which takes the place of the compositor's composing stick. When the operator presses the space key a wedge-shaped piece of metal comes into position between each word. When the line is nearly full the operator presses a handle and goes on with the next line.

But the machine, apparently working on its own in the most miraculous way, goes on to do a great many things. The matrices are taken from the box where they have been assembled and the space wedges are pressed up so that the line is exactly the right width. Then the matrices are pressed against a mould, molten metal is pumped against them, and the whole line of type, in one solid slug, is pushed out into a galley. The matrices which have been used are picked up by an arm and carried to the top of the machine, where you can see them slide along until each one comes to its own compartment, where it drops down into place as though it is alive and knows just where to go.

The Linotype is not the only machine for composing type. In 1897 another one was invented which produced single types and was therefore called a Monotype machine. Monotype machines are in two parts. At one the operator sits in front of a keyboard on which there are a large number of keys by means of which he can tap out words in seven different kinds of type—large capitals, small capitals, lower case (or small) letters, italics, and so on. And, of course, there are keys for numerals and for various other signs that appear in printed work.

Above the keyboard there is a roll of paper. As the operator strikes each key two or more holes are punched in the paper. As the key is released and returns to its original position the paper unwinds from its reel and moves on one step towards another reel on which it is gradually rewound. The holes on the paper are in different positions for each letter or sign on the keyboard, including the space bar, which is depressed between each word. When the line is nearly complete a bell rings. Meanwhile the machine has been registering the width of each letter and space in the line. The operator looks at a pointer against which are some figures. He presses keys on the keyboard corresponding to the figures, and that makes certain that the spaces will be adjusted in such a way that the line will be the right width.

At the end of any line, when enough of the work has been tapped out on the keyboard, the roll of paper is taken to the other machine—the Caster. As it unwinds again compressed air is released through each set of holes in turn and causes a matrix for the particular letter or sign to slip into place over a mould. Molten metal is pumped in, the mould is cooled at once with cold water, and the type letter is pushed out into a channel, where it lines up with its fellow letters. When a line is complete it is pushed out on to a galley.

The Monotype Casting machine is wonderful to watch, as it requires very little attention. Once it is started it continues to work away by itself until the paper roll is finished.

Composing machines such as the Linotype and Monotype save an enormous amount of time. When work is composed by hand the compositor not only has to set up the work, but after it is printed he has to distribute it—that is, he has to replace each letter and sign in its appropriate compartment in the case, and although compositors are wonderfully quick at the job it still takes a long time. When work that has been composed on the Linotype or Monotype machines is finished with the type is simply put back into the melting-pot to be melted down and used again for casting another line of type or another set of monotype letters.

However the work has been composed, once the galley proofs have been corrected and any necessary alterations have been made, the work has to be arranged in pages. The type in the galleys is divided up into the correct number of lines for each page, and such things as headings, footnotes and illustrations are inserted. Every page must be exactly the

Monotype typesetter (*left*) and type caster

Linotype machine for setting and casting type in a single operation

same size. When a page is ready it is tied up firmly with cord so that it won't fall apart, then the pages are arranged in the right order on a big, perfectly flat steel table, which is called the stone because in the past it used to be made of stone. The

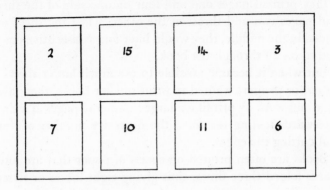

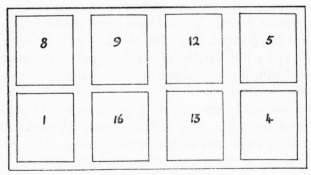

Sixteen-page imposition

man who arranges the pages, who does the imposition as it is called, is called the 'stone hand'.

Imposition seems rather a difficult job to people who are not used to it. As you know, each leaf or page of a book is printed on both sides, but the pages are not printed one by

N 193

one on sheets of paper just the right size. In very old pictures of sixteenth-century presses the printers are generally shown printing two pages side by side. They were using sheets of paper twice the size of the page. You can see, can't you, that if they printed pages one and four on one side of the sheet, and pages two and three on the other, when the sheet was folded in the middle, they would have four consecutive pages, and so on all through the book.

But when it became possible to use much larger sheets of paper, or printers wanted to print smaller books, they saved time and work by printing a large number of pages at a time, afterwards folding the sheet the necessary number of times and cutting the edges.

Books are often printed on sheets of paper that are afterwards folded three times, thus giving eight leaves or sixteen pages. Eight pages are printed on one side of the sheet and eight on the other, and you can see that if the pages of type were not correctly arranged in the first place the result would be a terrible muddle. The diagram shows you how the pages have to be arranged. If you like to take a sheet of paper and fold it into a little booklet of sixteen pages, and number the pages, you will see when you open it out again whether the diagram is right or not.

But you will have to fold the paper in a certain way. With the sheet flat on the table in front of you, you must fold the right-hand edge over to the left-hand edge, then the top edges down to the bottom edges, then the right-hand fold over to the left edges again. The man or woman doing the folding in a printing office holds a little bone implement (called a folder) in his right hand, folds the paper with his left hand, and runs the folder along the crease as it is made each time.

Actually printers often use very much larger sheets of paper and print a great many more than eight pages at a time. They have to work out very carefully just where each page must be placed on the stone.

When the type pages have been placed on the stone, correctly arranged, the stone-hand puts a steel frame with two cross-bars called a chase, around the whole lot of pages, and fixes metal or wood furniture around each page of the correct widths to give the necessary margins. Then between the outside furniture and the chase he fixes wedges, called quoins, which tighten up the pages of type and press them closely against the cross-bars so that no single piece of type can stir in the very slightest degree. He calls this 'locking up' the type. The whole arrangement of type pages, furniture, chase and quoins is called a 'forme', and it is so firm that it can be carried about without a single one of the many thousands of letters that make it up falling out of position.

The forme is now ready to be printed. For generations, as you know, the printing was done on a hand press, and hand presses are still used for some kinds of printing. In that case the forme is put on to a flat plate, called the bed of the press. A frame, called a tympan, is hinged on the bed, and the sheet of paper on which the printing is to be done is placed on this, and another frame, called a frisket, is folded down over it. After the forme has been inked the tympan with the sheet of paper in position is lowered on to the forme. Then the bed, which is set on runners, is made to slide back under an iron plate which is called a platen, the lever is pulled, and the platen descends on to the tympan. Then the platen is raised and the bed is drawn out from under it. The tympan is lifted, the frisket folded back, the printed sheet of paper is removed, and the whole series of actions is repeated for the next sheet.

You can see that to print thousands of copies of a full-length book by this method would take a very long time. So for most books modern printing machines are used such as Gutenberg and Caxton could never have dreamed of.

The steam-driven press that *The Times* used in 1814 was different in one very important way from the hand-presses. The platen (the part of the hand-press that descends on to the forme) was no longer a flat plate, but a cylinder which revolved as the bed on which the forme lay passed backwards and forwards under it. As the cylinder revolved it carried a sheet of paper round with it, which was pressed against the type. The type, for the first time, was inked automatically by passing under inked rollers. The sheets of paper still had to be fed into the machine by hand.

All kinds of things have happened to the printing press since those days. For one thing, of course, they are worked by electricity now and not by steam. The presses on which newspapers are printed are colossal great machines into which paper is fed at one end from great reels containing a mile or two of paper, and from which newspapers emerge at the other end, printed, folded, and even counted.

The presses on which books are printed are not so big or elaborate, but they are just as wonderful in their way. They print from twelve to fifteen hundred impressions in an hour, and with most of them now, it is no longer necessary for a man or woman to place each sheet of paper in position for the cylinder to carry it round. An automatic feeder takes up each sheet separately from a pile put in readiness, leads it carefully to the correct spot, and makes sure that the grippers have grasped it firmly, so that it will go on its way through the machine without any mishaps, until it comes out printed at the other end. These automatic feeders are wonderful to watch, for they seem sometimes to be acting as though they were human. If anything goes wrong—if a sheet of paper is crumpled or torn, or if it sticks to the sheet below, or if the grippers fail to grasp it—then the automatic feeder stops the machine, which it also does when the last sheet has been printed.

Of course, all these wonderful machines that have speeded up printing so enormously during the last century or so would be quite useless if each sheet of paper still had to be made by a man dipping a frame into a tub of milky fluid. Some of the best paper is still made by hand, but most of the paper we use for all sorts of purposes every day, and on which our books, magazines and newspapers are printed, is made by machinery.

The material used for making paper in the early days was usually linen rags. But as the demand for paper became greater, the supply of rags began to run out, and men tried to find some other material that would serve the purpose. Early in the nineteenth century straw was tried, but it was not very satisfactory. Wood, too, was tried at about the same time, and that was more successful—in fact, it is the material from which cheaper papers such as newsprint are made to-day, and huge forests are being destroyed in order to supply us all with our daily newspapers.

Another material that has been used a great deal, especially in Great Britain, is a kind of grass that grows round the shores of the Mediterranean called esparto grass. Experiments are still being carried on to find materials from which paper can be made cheaply and easily.

The first paper-making machine was invented by a Frenchman in 1798, and was brought into England in 1803. It has been improved, of course, since, and enormous machines now make a long ribbon of paper, several yards wide, which winds itself on to huge reels holding as much as two miles of paper.

The material from which the paper is to be made has first to be washed and, in the case of rags, any oddments such as buttons removed. Then it has to be beaten, to break it up into fibres. If wood is being used it can be broken down in two ways—either by pressing it against a revolving grindstone, in water, until it is shredded up, or by mixing it with different chemicals, according to the kind of paper required. The first way is the cheapest and is used for making newspaper.

Esparto grass, after being cleaned, is boiled with caustic soda. Then, like the other materials, it is beaten in a machine that breaks down the fibres, until a thin pulp is formed.

The pulp passes into a large vat in which it is kept constantly moving so that the fibres shall not settle. Finally it reaches a wide, continuously moving belt of woven wire, through which the water drains away, leaving the fibres on the top. The belt shakes about from side to side, so that the fibres do not all lie in the same direction. After travelling some distance the wire carries the still wet pulp under some rollers, which squeeze out more water. Then the material, which by this time begins to look like paper, passes from the wire belt on to one made of felt, and through more rollers, when the fibres are pressed more firmly together and more water is squeezed out. Then it passes over heated rollers to give it a smooth surface, and is finally wound on to the huge reels.

After it is made paper often has to be finished in various ways, according to the purpose for which it is to be used. The shiny paper, for instance, on which photographs in books are often reproduced, and which is called 'art paper', is coated with glazed china-clay. And, of course, the paper has to be cut into sheets of certain definite sizes, unless it is to be used for printing newspapers. Then it is fed into the huge machines direct from the reel.

The sizes into which paper for book printing is cut are known by certain names. 'Imperial', for instance, is twenty-two inches by thirty inches, 'Royal' is twenty inches by twenty-five, 'Medium' is eighteen and a half inches by twenty-three and a half, 'Demy' seventeen and a half inches by twenty-two and a half, and 'Crown' fifteen inches by twenty.

CHAPTER XXII

★

How Pictures are Printed

During the last hundred and fifty years not only have new ways of composing and printing been developed, but new ways of reproducing pictures, too. You remember that in the early days of printing, pictures were usually printed from wood blocks. In the eighteenth century copperplate engravings were very popular, and towards the end of the century Thomas Bewick developed a new way of making wood-engravings.

But during the nineteenth century photography was invented and improved, and this led in time to a way of printing pictures that did away with the necessity for cutting or engraving all pictures by hand. It was discovered that a photograph of the drawing to be reproduced could be printed on a specially prepared zinc plate. The plate was then put into a bath of acid, which bit away the zinc background, leaving the lines of the drawing raised, as in a wood block. The zinc plate could then be mounted on wood to make it 'type-high', and could be printed from in the ordinary way.

A great many of the black and white illustrations we see in our books are reproduced in this way—from 'line-blocks' as we call them. Sometimes coloured pictures are printed by means of line-blocks, too, but in that case a separate block has to be made for each colour, and the blocks are printed one after the other, great care being taken to see that each colour falls in the right place—that the picture 'registers', as printers call it. I am sure you have seen cheap, badly printed pictures in which the colours overlap, or stick out over the edge of the drawing.

A line-block can print only one colour at a time. It cannot print different shades of grey, or lighter and darker tones of a colour. For a long time men in different parts of the world were experimenting to find a way of reproducing photo-

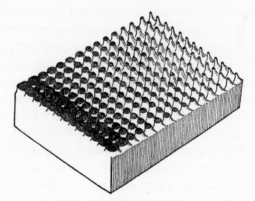

Part of a half-tone block

graphs and paintings with all their varying tones. At last they discovered that they could do it by photographing the original through a glass screen which was criss-crossed with fine black lines, so that it was covered with tiny squares. The photograph appeared on the negative as a number of dots, large and close together, or small and farther apart, according to the darkness or lightness of any particular part of the original picture. When the zinc plate on which the photograph was printed had been etched in the acid bath it, too, appeared as a number of raised dots, from which a print could be taken which reproduced the varying tones of the original. A block made in this way is called a half-tone block.

The squares on the screen can be very tiny—as many as two hundred and twenty-five to the inch—or fairly large—about sixty-five to the inch. The smaller they are the finer the reproduction will be, and the better the paper must be on which it is printed. For the photographs that appear in newspapers a fairly coarse screen is used. If you examine a newspaper photograph through a magnifying glass you will find that you can see the dots of which the picture is made up quite easily.

The next step was to make half-tone blocks that would reproduce pictures in colour. As I expect you know, all colours are made by mixing the three primary colours, red, yellow and blue, in different proportions. The early experimenters discovered that it was possible to photograph one colour only in a picture, using filters that would prevent the camera from photographing either of the other two. So by making three half-tone blocks, one for all the yellow, one for all the blue, and one for all the red in a picture (with, perhaps, another block for black if necessary), and printing them one on top of another, they were able to reproduce coloured pictures in all their various tones.

Of course, these different ways of reproducing pictures have been improved since they were introduced, and they are still being improved as new discoveries are being made. And there are other ways of reproducing pictures, but those I have described are the most commonly used.

Other things connected with the making of a book are done by machine nowadays, as well as the composing of the type, the printing and the reproduction of the pictures.

The big sheets on which a number of pages have been printed are put into a machine that folds them in the right way. Each section of the book has a little letter (or sometimes a figure) at the bottom of the first page, which helps the people who assemble them together to get them in the right order. If you look through a book you will find the little letter at regular intervals according to the size of the sections. Probably it will be on every sixteenth page. The sections are often called signatures.

The signatures are arranged in the right order, and any separate illustrations are inserted in the proper places. Then the sections are taken to a machine which stitches them all together, after which the book is put into a machine that presses the pages up tightly.

The next machine is called the guillotine. It holds the book firmly while a knife descends and cuts the fore edge to make it straight and even, and then two other knives cut the other two edges, the head and tail. Then the book is put spine downwards on a machine that carries it along and puts a coat of glue over the spine. After it has had time to dry a bit the book goes to a machine that gives the spine the round shape that the backs of books have when they are shut.

The next machine does a great many things. It carries the books along from one stopping-place to another, and at each spot a different action is performed. At the first the spine of the book receives another coat of glue; at the second a piece of loosely woven linen material called mull is cut off a roll and is applied to the spine; at the next a roller presses the mull on to the spine; at the next another coat of glue is put over the mull; at the next a strip of paper is cut off and put over the mull, and finally a roller presses the paper firmly into place.

In the meantime another machine has been making the cover, or case as it is usually called. You remember that for generations books were almost always bound in leather. But about 1825 a printer named William Pickering used cloth for the first time, and by degrees the new material became popular until, now, our books are nearly always covered in cloth. Pickering used calico, but binders of to-day use all kinds of material.

The case-making machine is supplied with a roll of material of the right width. As the roll unwinds the cloth passes over a roller which gives it a coat of glue. Then the machine drops two boards, for the two sides of the book, on to the cloth, and a strip of stiff paper in between them for the spine, knives cut the cloth between each book, and the machine turns the edges of the cloth in over the boards and the stiff paper, and presses it firmly into position.

The case is then taken to another machine which prints the title of the book and the author's and publisher's names on the spine.

Then the cases and the books are put in a casing machine which puts a coat of paste over the mull and the endpapers on each book, and presses one of the cases over it.

The books are now put into a press for several hours until they are dry and firm. Then they are wrapped in their coloured paper jackets, which will serve to protect the cloth covers. They also make the books look attractive and individual, so that they will stand out from other books in a shop window, and, probably, make you want to buy them.

CHAPTER XXIII

★

How We Got Our Libraries

When the first hand-presses started to turn out books in hundreds instead of one at a time as the scribes had done, books came within the reach of far more people than ever before. But even then there were still vast numbers of people who scarcely ever saw a book, and who could not afford to buy one if they did.

Then came the power presses, worked first by steam and then by electricity, and later the composing machines—the Linotype and the Monotype—all of which made it possible for books to be produced in such numbers that there were plenty for everybody. So that now, even though we are still suffering from paper shortages and other effects of the last war, we can go into a bookshop and buy or order almost any book we want, and usually get it—though we may have to wait a little while for it.

But perhaps you say—'That's all very well. But we haven't all got money enough to buy all the books we should like to have, and we haven't room for them in our homes even if we could buy them.'

Those two problems, or something like them, have faced book-lovers at all times. But we who are alive to-day are far luckier than most people were even a hundred years ago. We may not be able to *buy* the book we want, but we can almost certainly read it if we really want to. Very few people to-day are completely out of reach of a library of some kind.

Of course, there were libraries long before there were printed books. You have already read quite a lot about them. But they were usually libraries belonging to private people—book-lovers who had gone to a lot of trouble to collect books and have them properly cared for. Or else they were libraries belonging to colleges or monasteries or cathedrals, and only the people connected with the particular body could use the books.

The monastic libraries were scattered or destroyed at the time of the dissolution of the monasteries by Henry VIII, and some of the other libraries suffered, too, during the sixteenth and seventeenth centuries.

One of the most famous of the university libraries is the Bodleian Library at Oxford. The oldest part of the Bodleian is called 'Duke Humphrey's Library'. That is because Humphrey, Duke of Gloucester, the fourth son of Henry IV, gave a collection of manuscript books to Oxford early in the fifteenth century, and an upper floor was built over the Divinity School to house them. In a letter to Duke Humphrey one of the university scribes wrote: 'We wish you could see the students bending over your books in their greediness and thirst for knowledge.' So the Duke's gift was certainly appreciated.

But in Edward VI's time, over a hundred years later, ideas had changed a great deal, and just as the Catholics in some countries tried to destroy all Protestant books, so the Protestants in England set about destroying all books that they considered 'Popish' or Catholic. Many rare and valuable books were destroyed all over the country. Duke Humphrey's Library suffered very severely. A large number of the books were burnt, and others were sold to bookbinders for their covers, or to other tradesmen as waste. The destruction was so complete that only four or five of the Duke's original books have ever been found. The shelves and desks were used for firewood.

Towards the end of the sixteenth century a much-travelled scholar named Sir Thomas Bodley settled down in Oxford and became interested in the library. He tells us that he made up his mind that 'I could not busy myself to better purpose than by reducing that place (which then in every part lay ruined and waste) to the public use of students'.

He superintended the refitting of the library—the building of a fine new roof, the designing and fitting of reading-desks and benches, and the searching out and buying of books from booksellers all over Europe. His library was opened on 8th November 1602. Although books were now printed and so were not so valuable as they had been when there might be only a few copies of any particular book in existence, they were all still chained, and continued to be for generations.

Bodley left his money to the library he had founded. Ever since his death in 1613 the library has continued to grow, partly by the purchase of books and partly because other collectors have left their valuable collections to the Bodleian from time to time. One scholar and writer who did this was John Selden, who died in 1654. A part of the Bodleian that is built on to one end of Duke Humphrey's Library is called the 'Selden End'. When John Selden's books were being sorted and examined at Oxford several pairs of spectacles were found which Selden had put into the books as bookmarks and forgotten. Spectacles were worn in the seventeenth century, but they were supplied in a very casual sort of way. A certain Lord Ferrers wrote to a relation in London asking him to buy two pairs of the best spectacles for him, and said, 'You know my age and therefore want no further direction'!

The original chamber—Duke Humphrey's Library—is now only a small part of the whole Bodleian Library. In it the books are still arranged on presses set at right angles to the walls, just as they were in Bodley's time, though they are no longer chained. From about the seventeenth century, as new wings were built, it became the custom for the first time to place shelves against the walls, from floor to ceiling, and to have a gallery built about half-way up the room, from which people could reach the upper shelves.

The Bodleian now possesses about 700,000 volumes, and 32,000 manuscripts, and among its books are some of the most valuable in the world.

Cambridge University was not so lucky as Oxford, as it did not have a Sir Thomas Bodley to give it such a good start. Nevertheless, it has had a number of generous benefactors, and it has grown from fifty-two volumes (probably kept in chests or cupboards) mentioned in a list made in 1425, until, like the Bodleian, it contains many thousands of books occupying a large building. Cambridge University stopped chaining their books after 1626.

Among the private people who collected large numbers of books in the Middle Ages, and after, were the Kings of England. Sometimes they bought books, and sometimes they had them presented to them, or other collectors left their collections to the Royal Library when they died. You remember the priceless Codex Alexandrinus was presented to James I by the Patriarch of Constantinople.

In 1759 the British Museum and its library were opened—not in the huge building where they are now but in a London mansion called Montagu House. The library consisted of the books from the Royal Library, which George II presented to it, and several other collections that had been made by other book-lovers. As time went on many other large and valuable collections were bought, and the library grew enormously. In the middle of last century the museum and library moved into the large new building which it still occupies.

The British Museum Library now contains over two million books. It has an enormous circular reading-room which is very famous. There are shelves all round the walls, and the desks at which readers sit to read and write radiate like the spokes of a wheel from the central space in which the librarians work. The books on the shelves are only a very few of the vast number the library owns; the others are stored on miles of shelves away in the background behind the reading-room, and have to be found and brought to the reader by one of the assistants.

The great catalogue of the British Museum Library fills something like fourteen hundred volumes. The volumes are like very large ledgers with blank pages on to which printed slips are pasted, in the right alphabetical order, giving particulars of each book. Fresh slips are constantly being added as new books come in.

The volumes of the catalogue are arranged on low bookcases which form almost a complete circle between the central space where the assistants are and the radiating desks at which the readers sit. Each reader has to find the book he wants in the catalogue and then fill up a form giving details about it, and its library number, and the number of his seat, after which he sits and waits until it is brought to him.

Every year the library grows bigger. By law a copy of every book that is published in England, Ireland, Scotland and Wales has to be sent to six libraries in the British Isles. The libraries are the British Museum, the Bodleian at Oxford, the Cambridge University Library, the National Library of Scotland, the Library of Trinity College, Dublin, and the National Library of Wales at Aberystwyth.

The libraries you have just been reading about were very valuable indeed for those people who had the right to use them. But before the eighteenth century there were very few libraries for the ordinary people who were not connected with a university or other learned society, and who were not wealthy enough to buy books for themselves. Some churches had a few books, as well as the chained Bible, which were kept for the use of parishioners, so that, in a way, they formed the first public libraries. Then during the seventeenth century a few towns started libraries. One of the very first was started in the Free Grammar School at Coventry in 1601 and existed until about 1913, when the Governors of the school sold all that remained of it. Another early one was started at Norwich in 1603.

Usually libraries like these came into existence because some citizen, at his death, left his books to his native town for the use of the townspeople. But unfortunately such people very seldom left any money so that new books could be bought and the libraries kept up to date, and a librarian paid to look after the books. So very often, after a few years, people ceased to read the books and the library was no longer used or cared for.

Then, early in the eighteenth century, it occurred to someone that people who could not afford to buy many books might be glad to pay a small sum for the chance to read them. Whoever he was, he was quite right, and the circulating libraries, as they were called were very popular indeed, and still are. One of the first was started by a poet named Allan Ramsey in his bookshop in Edinburgh, and we are told that his shop became the haunt of all the most prominent citizens of the town, including Sir Walter Scott, the author of *Ivanhoe* and many other books that you may have read.

Of course, there were people who did not approve of the circulating libraries, and who said that the books they supplied were 'villainous and profane' and that they would put bad ideas into people's heads. But the circulating libraries

o   209

continued to flourish, and by 1770 there was one in nearly every town of any size in Britain.

But there were still a great many people in the country who never saw any books at all, and who could not have read them even if they had. There were hardly any schools for the poor, and children started work very young—at seven or eight years old—and worked for very long hours, so that most of them grew up unable to read or write.

Some people became very worried by this state of things, and one of them, Robert Raikes of Gloucester, in 1780, started a Sunday-school where children could learn not only about religion but to read as well. Other people followed his example, and before his death in 1811, Sunday-schools had spread all over England. Grown-up people went to them as well as children.

Early in the nineteenth century two societies were formed for the purpose of educating the children of poor people. One was called 'The National Society for the Education of the Poor' and the head of it was a Church of England clergyman named Andrew Bell, and the other was 'The British and Foreign School Society' of which the head was a Quaker named Joseph Lancaster.

Thousands of schools were started all over the country by one or other of these societies, but they were not a bit like the schools you are used to. All the children worked in one room, and there would usually be only one master. But the schools were run on what was called the Lancasterian system, although it had really been practised earlier, in India, by Andrew Bell, who had written a description of it when he came back to England. By this system the master taught something to a few children, and they then taught what they had learnt to the others. In this way a great many of the children of poor parents, who paid a few pence a week, were taught to read and write.

In 1832 Parliament, for the first time, made a grant of money so that schools could be built, though it was not until 1870 that a law was passed which said that all children *must* attend school.

As more people learnt to read there grew up, of course, a greater demand for books. There were not nearly enough libraries. In some places working people banded together to help themselves to get a better education. They arranged for educated men to lecture to them, and they formed collections of books for their own use. The associations they formed were called Mechanics' Institutes. The first was started in Glasgow early in the nineteenth century, but by 1863 there were about seven hundred in England alone.

But all these different libraries only reached certain people. Then in the middle of the nineteenth century three men— William Brotherton and William Ewart, who were Members of Parliament, and Edward Edwards, who was a librarian in the British Museum Library—began working to convince Parliament that Public Libraries, open free, ought to be established in England and paid for out of the rates. There was a lot of opposition, but at last, in 1850, an Act was passed which allowed boroughs to collect a rate of a half-penny in the pound and use the money to build a library, if the people of the borough agreed that they wanted one.

This was certainly a start, but only a very feeble one. The money raised by the halfpenny rate was not nearly enough. And in any case, the borough councils were not allowed to spend any of the money on *books*! They could buy or build their library, but to stock it with books they had to beg from book-lovers, or hope that well-wishers would leave their collections to them when they died.

In 1855 an Act was passed which raised the rate that could be levied from a halfpenny to one penny, and which said that the council of any town with five thousand inhabitants might call a meeting of its householders and if two-thirds agreed that they wanted a library, then the rate could be levied and the library built. And the councils were allowed to buy books out of the money.

But the money was still not nearly enough, so it is not surprising that public libraries spread over the country very slowly. Norwich was the first town to call a meeting and decide to take advantage of the 1850 Act, and it did it within one month of the Act being passed. But the library was not ready for a long time, and the first free public library actually to be opened under the Act was the one at Manchester. It was opened on 2nd September 1852, and many notable people were present, including Charles Dickens, Bulwer Lytton and William Thackeray.

There would have been even fewer free public libraries opened during the seventy years after the Act was passed if it had not been for a very generous man named Andrew Carnegie. He was born in Scotland in 1835, and went to America with his parents. He got work with the Pennsylvania Railroad Co. and lived in Pittsburg. There he and some other boys were befriended by a Col. Anderson, who allowed them to use his library. Andrew Carnegie was so grateful that he vowed if ever he had money he would spend it in establishing free libraries. A time came when he had got money—so much of it that he was one of the richest men in the world. And he kept his vow. All over England and Scotland there are libraries which came into existence largely because Andrew Carnegie gave the money for them to be built, his only conditions being that the town provided the land free, and undertook to support the library after it was built by adopting the Act and levying the rate. By the time Carnegie died in 1919 he had given away over seventy million pounds.

By another Act passed in 1919 Councils were no longer

restricted to a rate of one penny, and they could spend whatever they thought necessary on their libraries. So at last
librarians were able to introduce the improvements that
some of them had been thinking about for years.

One of the things they had been thinking about was
children's libraries. Some of the day-schools had had libraries
since 1878. The books were changed every six months. But
the public libraries had never had enough money even for
the work they wanted to do for grown-up people. Some of
them managed to have a few shelves for children's books, but
that was not very much good as children were not allowed
into the buildings until they were fourteen. Some of them
tried to do a little more. At Manchester, in 1861, a room was
set aside for children, but it was a rather comfortless underground room, furnished with a long table and some school
forms. There were no books to be seen, but a book would be
handed over the counter to any child who had the courage to
go in and ask for one.

Cardiff and other places experimented with the idea of
providing separate rooms for children, but they were generally reading-rooms, not lending libraries from which children
could borrow books to take home. And there were no specially trained assistants who worked only with children and
who knew all about children's books.

Although the books in some of these reading-rooms could
be seen and asked for they could not be taken from the
shelves by the children themselves. But in this the children
were no worse off than their parents, who also had to ask for
the book they wanted, when an assistant would go and get it
for them if it was in the library. The 'open access' system, as it
is called, by which borrowers can go to the shelves and choose
books for themselves, was first introduced at Clerkenwell Public Library in 1894, when James Duff Brown was librarian,
and some other librarians did not approve of the idea at all.

The first children's library to have a separate building of its own, with its own staff and catalogue, was opened in 1882 in Nottingham, when J. Potter Briscoe was librarian, and a Member of Parliament named Samuel Morley gave £500 for the purpose. As time passed many other public libraries —those for instance at Liverpool, Chelsea, Islington and Hampstead—provided libraries for children. But it was not until after the Act of 1919, which allowed Councils to spend more money on their libraries, that it became possible for librarians to provide really complete children's libraries with special furniture and a really good supply of books for children of all ages. A typical early example that provided just as much for children as the adult library did for grown-ups was opened at Croydon in 1920, when Mr. Berwick Sayers was librarian. He had only a single hall seventy feet long for his children's library, but he managed to arrange it in such a way that the children had a reference library, a lending library, a reading-room, a lecture-room, and a newspaper-room.

Since that time most libraries of any size have managed to open a children's library. In many of them the children can not only borrow books to take home, but they can sit in the library to do their homework and can consult reference books if they want to. And there are librarians trained especially for children's libraries, who know all about children's books and can give help and advice when it is wanted. The librarians often arrange lectures, or talks about books, or story-reading and story-telling periods on certain days during the week.

There are very few people nowadays who cannot borrow books if they really want to. If their own library has not got the book they want they can ask for it and it will be obtained for them from some other library under a scheme called the Central Library Scheme. Even in tiny villages there is often a library under the County Library Scheme, perhaps in the school or in somebody's house, and the books are changed every few months. And some counties have arranged for vans, beautifully fitted up with shelves and well stocked with books, to travel round the country and call at isolated farms and houses. If people want special books they can order them and the travelling library will bring them next time it calls. There are libraries, too, for the blind, from which books in Braille are sent to blind people by post and changed once a month.

How different all this is from the days when monks patiently copied books word by word, and a book was such a rare and precious thing that it had to be kept locked in a chest or cupboard, or chained firmly to a desk.

Now books, magazines, and newspapers are so plentiful that one of the most difficult problems librarians have to solve is how to find room to store them all. This is especially so in the case of the six British libraries that receive copies of every book that is published in Great Britain, and similar libraries in other countries.

One way of preserving books and magazines that has been tried is by photographing the book page by page on to a narrow strip of cine-film, which rolls up and fits into a small box. The film can then be run through a special machine which the reader looks into, and sees the writing enlarged to its full size again. Perhaps some time in the future our libraries will consist not of books as we know them but of vast numbers of tiny boxes, each carefully labelled, and instead of bringing a book home under our arm we shall bring one of the little boxes home in our pockets. And all our homes will be equipped with the necessary reading-machine, just as they are now fitted up with radio sets and telephones.

I don't suppose the idea appeals to you very much. Neither does it to me, for most of us enjoy the look and feel of a good book almost as much as we enjoy reading what is printed in it. But everything changes, and we have seen that books are no exception. At different times they have taken many forms. They have been clay tablets, papyrus rolls, parchment codices and paper books as we know them. They have been scratched, painted, written and printed in an endless number of ways. The story of the book has been a very long one, and it is still going on, and will continue to go on as long as human beings think and feel and want to pass their thoughts and feelings on to other men and women.

Index

Index

Index